EFFECTIVE
USE OF
CHURCH
SPACE

EFFECTIVE USE OF CHURCH SPACE

**Church Buildings
in a Time of
Energy Shortages
and High Costs**

RALPH L. BELKNAP

Judson Press® Valley Forge

EFFECTIVE USE OF CHURCH SPACE

Bible quotations in this volume are in accordance with the Revised Standard Version of the Bible, copyrighted 1946, 1952, 1971, 1973 © by the Division of Christian Education of the National Council of the Churches of Christ in the United States of America, and are used by permission.

Library of Congress Cataloging in Publication Data

Belknap, Ralph L.
  Effective use of church space.

  Bibliography: p. 169.
  1. Church facilities—Planning. I. Title.
  BV604.B37   254'.7   78-14911
  ISBN 0-8170-0764-4

The name JUDSON PRESS is registered as a trademark in the U.S. Patent Office. Printed in the U.S.A. ✌

Acknowledgments

This writing would have been impossible without the participation, experience, and expertise of my colleagues on the American Baptist Extension Corporation staff. Their cooperation in allowing time to write, responding to the content, and contributing original ideas is deeply appreciated. Thanks must also be expressed to others who assisted, such as John Anderson and Gary Sharp, who drew illustrations and gave ideas, and Don Erickson and Robert Hershberger who contributed to the chapter on conserving energy. Throughout, I have never felt like a soloist, but rather part of a rewarding team effort.

Ralph L. Belknap

Contents

Introduction   9

1 The Planning Process   13

2 Six Planning Options for Churches   31

3 Flexible Space   53

4 Conserving Energy   75

5 Solar Energy for Churches   93

6 Beautiful Church Buildings   113

7 What Can the Church Afford?   123

8 Raising and Borrowing Funds   139

Appendix A Survey Report Outline   153

Appendix B Formula for Energy Efficiency Ratio   159

Appendix C Checklist for Reducing Fuel Use
in Church Buildings   161

Appendix D Cost Pay-back Period   163

Appendix E Construction Budget   165

Selected Bibliography   169

Index   173

Introduction

The major purpose of this book is to point to some specific ways that churches may make better use of their resources so that more can be utilized to meet human needs. The church was commissioned to confront people with their need for God. Jesus said, "Go into all the world and preach the gospel to the whole creation" (Mark 16:15). The purpose of the church is also to meet the physical needs of people. Christians are to feed the hungry, visit the sick, clothe the naked (Matthew 25:34-40). Jesus exemplified the necessity of caring for both body and soul. At the heart of Christianity there is no separation, no dualism. The church must continue this ministry to the total needs of humankind.

In order to carry out this ministry in contemporary times, some enabling, supporting equipment seems to be required, such as buildings and land. However, continual guard must be maintained to make certain that the equipment does not handicap or even prevent the ministry. Imagine a climber who has a tremendous desire to conquer a high mountain. In preparation for the assault, every conceivable type of mountain-climbing equipment is purchased. But, on the morning of the attempt, the climber cannot even pass the 3,000-foot level because the equipment is so heavy that exhaustion sets in. The major goal is not achieved because the equipment for doing it got in the way.

This same problem can be experienced by the church. The tools, the equipment, may be given such a high priority that the ministry is not accomplished. So much energy and money are spent on such equipment as buildings, land, and utilities that relatively few resources remain for use in fulfilling the real purpose of the church. A thorough review of church budgets would reveal many with overhead expenditures taking a large part of the budget.

Most religious institutions in America have taken on those same characteristics of consumption and waste which are a part of contemporary society. Instead of prophetically challenging these characteristics, churches have incorporated them into their standard mode of operation. Too many have been duped into believing that "bigger is better." Churches have felt that they should match the surrounding affluent society by spending large sums of money on land, buildings, and creature comforts. Such equipment, plus the resources necessary for utilities and maintenance, has left comparatively little for ministries to the needs of people. It is no wonder that many questions are asked about the real goals and priorities of the church. Such inquiries require a thoughtful response.

Genesis 1:26-30 records that humankind is the pinnacle, the ultimate achievement of God's creation. Humans are to have "dominion over all the earth." This passage has been interpreted in diverse ways. To some, it means living in harmony with nature in such a manner that benefits are derived without artificial aids or altering the delicate balance of the eco-system. The environment is left in as good condition as, or better than, it was found. Native Americans generally exemplified this life-style even though they had not read Genesis.

To others, many of whom are familiar with the scriptural passage, having dominion has meant controlling, exploiting, depleting, even devastating the earth. Strip-mining without reclamation is an example. Instead of living in harmony with nature, artificial environments have been constructed with many natural resources necessary to control and manipulate those spaces. Most people would probably find themselves between these extremes, enjoying the luxuries of life while being mainly indifferent to any negative consequences of their life-style.

It is likely that the most accurate interpretation of the Genesis passage is that dominion really means responsibility "to maintain the perfection of creation," not defile or destroy it. "Man over nature is man under God."[1] Humanity has the responsibility of exercising

[1] Phyllis Trible, "Ancient Priests and Modern Polluters," *Foundations*, vol. 17, no. 2 (April-June, 1974), pp. 161-162.

dominion ONLY within the context of God's love and goodness. All of the earth's resources belong to God. The Creator has prior ownership rights. Human beings are but stewards of these precious gifts for a brief moment of time. Human control is, obviously, limited, but what there is should serve the laws of nature and nature's God, not oppose, circumvent, or ignore them. Depriving future generations of natural resources and, perhaps, life itself, is neither goodness nor love. "Pollution results from man's disobedience, not from his dominion."[2] (Even if, by some miracle, resources were unlimited, how Christians treat the earth would still be a relevant issue.)

Citizens of the United States of America have a special responsibility in this regard. Prosperity has come because the Creator gave more natural resources to this land than to most. ". . . to whom much is given, of him will much be required . . ." (Luke 12:48). Christians in the United States must discover how to handle this major stewardship responsibility. Americans use energy at approximately six times the rate of the rest of the people in the world. Calculating the amount of energy that the average human being can produce and the amount of energy each American now uses, the equivalent of twenty slaves are working for each citizen!

By living more simply, more in harmony with nature, the use of natural resources would decrease. Since the amount of such resources on Spaceship Earth is definitely limited, conservation is important. Conservation alone will not guarantee that those living in underdeveloped countries would receive more of the necessities and some of the luxuries of life, but it would at least make that kind of sharing possible. American demand for natural resources raises prices on the world market, making it more difficult for others to obtain them. "Am I my brother's keeper?" was the question asked by Cain (Genesis 4:9). While American churches and the government have usually been at the forefront in responding to emergency needs around the world, perhaps the greatest disaster is now here and it is still not fully recognized. Overconsumption leads beyond resource depletion to ultimate, inevitable death. Americans are our brothers'/sisters' keeper, both at home and abroad. Having been given much, there is a great responsibility. What will be the response of the stewards of God's earth?

Certainly the beginning point is for informed church members to

[2] *Ibid.,* pp. 162-163.

use far more wisely the resources of land, water, air, material goods, fossil fuels, and buildings for which they have some stewardship responsibility. This responsibility relates to life in the home, the factory or office, the city or county of residence, and the church. More than simply a matter of economics, conservation is a philosophy, a life-style, even a matter of survival. The gasoline shortage of 1973–1974 and the heating fuel shortage of the severe 1976–1977 winter have only served to underscore this need. Some form of coal, oil, or natural gas power is required to make and operate almost every item one could place on a list of "essentials" for daily life. And most of these resources are fast disappearing. All the basic life-sustaining materials are God's gift to humankind. In simple but theological terms, this means that knowingly to waste or underutilize these gifts is to commit sin; to conserve and stretch and recycle them is to do God's will.

This philosophy could be interpreted as being anti-scientific or even anti-progress. It is not meant to be either. The fertile human mind which has unlocked many secrets of the universe is a creation of God to be celebrated. In ethical terms, new inventions and discoveries are neither "good" nor "bad." They are neutral, amoral. The key is in how knowledge is used by humankind. Fire can warm families in winter, cook food, or be used in destructive ways. Nuclear energy can generate electricity or destroy persons and property.

Now that more is known about the physical limitations of the earth, wise choices may be made. The Stone Age need not return! Alternative sources of energy can be developed, such as sun and wind, to provide creature comforts and a high standard of living without destroying the planet. Pollution can be reduced, public transportation improved, expansion of cities made more humane. A more natural technology is here if we want to use it. E. F. Schumacher has called it "technology with a human face."[3]

Furthermore, it is not too late for churches and Christians to make those ethical, moral decisions which are more consistent with the teachings of Scripture than many of our past decisions. It is not a matter of retreat versus progress. It is a matter of choosing those options which are more just to the worldwide family of nations and as harmonious as possible with the ecology of the earth which has been given to us.

[3] E. F. Schumacher, *Small Is Beautiful* (New York: Harper & Row, Publishers, 1973), p. 138. (See Part II, Section 5, for a penetrating discussion of this subject.)

The
Planning Process 1

Careful planning is necessary if the church is to direct more of its limited resources toward meeting the needs of humanity. Christians do not love and worship a capricious deity. Genesis, chapter 1, tells us that God's first act, the act of creation, was orderly and consistent. The universe has the kind of mathematical symmetry which allows astronomers to chart the courses of stars, planets, and moons with near-perfect accuracy. Both the telescope and the microscope reveal God as the Omnipotent Creator who pays as much attention to the details in atoms as to the courses of the galaxies.

Humanity is part of God's divine plan. In a tremendous act of trust, God created people with minds and wills that are free. Humankind often abuses that freedom, however, and tends to be capricious, unpredictable, rebellious. God wishes otherwise. Hope lies in the fact that sometimes people do see the vision and become selfless rather than selfish, supportive rather than critical. The example is there, pulling constantly. Although humanity is an enigma, God is thoroughly consistent in his efforts to love, forgive, inspire, uplift.

Likewise, God has set forth, in every aspect of creation, an example of efficient, orderly planning to those who are concerned about the stewardship of church resources. As in all other subjects, God's planning is a high example, but that fact does not relieve Christians of the obligation to try. Planning is a reflection of God's universe and of God. Our response is expected but is not achieved as often as it could be.

Why Plan?

Church members have the tremendous opportunity of being co-creators with God, of forming what their lives and their congregations become. However, rather than shaping the future, the temptation is to follow the procedure of reacting to immediate pressures both from within the congregation and from the community. Business meetings then become emergency sessions dealing with survival rather than creative events leading to ministry. There is a better way! Ask the church that knows. To form is much more stimulating and productive than to react.

To react means to waste natural, financial, and human resources. A church in the Midwest found itself in a rapidly growing community. Expanded physical facilities were needed, and there was little time to "waste" in planning. An architect was employed; blueprints were prepared, contracts accepted, and construction started before all the facts were in. The designed space turned out to be larger than the budget would allow. But footings were already poured and structural steel was in place! There was no alternative other than finishing as much of the building as possible and completing the rest later. Several years passed in the meantime, however, with lonely steel I-beams rusting in the sun.

In a city serving as home for a large, prestigious university, a national denominational body decided to build a student center. Reacting to a particular need that was in vogue at the time, an expensive structure was erected to meet one specific program requirement. Within less than five years, that program was passé. Because of the inflexible construction, the obsolete five-year-old building was offered for sale. Several more years were to pass before the property was sold and the church was able to recover its investment.

Planning has always been necessary, but never more so than now. Change is the watchword of the day. The fact that there is rapid change should never be an excuse for nonplanning. To the contrary, the only way to deal constructively with change is to recognize its inevitability and to have several options in mind so that the best one can be implemented when needed. This is the way a business remains competitive and profitable. It is the way human beings stay relatively healthy in the face of traumatic experiences. It is also the way that the church must operate if it is to be a major positive factor in the life of its members and of the world.

Serious planning is certainly not the easy option. It takes considerable time, effort, and resources. It is much less strenuous to drift than to plan. However, remember that indecision is, in itself, a decision. Imagine a man on a raft floating leisurely down a river. He becomes hungry and wonders if he should stop at the next town to eat dinner. But then he feels a nap coming on, so slumbers long enough for the raft to carry him far past the next town. He awakens with a jolt as his raft hits a rock. He is very hungry now, but his indecision has definitely decided for him that he will not have dinner in that town back up the river.

The church is moving forward in time, more quickly every year, or at least it seems that way. Without adequate planning, changes occur at such a pace that some possibilities which looked good a few years ago are now not even available. By not deciding, the church has decided *against* those options! Others are available, to be sure, and perhaps as many or more than before, but they are now different options and sometimes less appealing.

Serious planning takes into account the rapidity of change, the fact that indecision is a decision, and also the sobering realization that the best projections and goals are far from perfect. Not too many years ago, a major religious group had the audacity to project a 100-year plan for their rural congregations!

While new buildings can survive from 40 to 150 years, the programs which they now house may have a duration as short as six weeks. In its lifetime, an urban church building could be used by three, four, or more different congregations. Perhaps five years is about the longest time programs can realistically be planned; so buildings need to be flexible or they may rapidly become obsolete.

Although the best of planning is imperfect, it is far better than the alternative of nonplanning. Granted, it is much more difficult these days to make decisions. Life has been enormously complicated by technological advances, overpopulation, rapid communication and transportation, accelerating social change, and many other factors. For many years, a man had a job sorting potatoes. He was stationed at the end of a long conveyor belt, with a basket on each side. The basket on the right was for large potatoes, the one on the left for small ones. One day on the job, he lost control of himself and had a complete nervous breakdown. As he was being led away, he was heard to mumble, "decisions, decisions." If his job led to trauma, then think about those confronted with complicated decisions today!

There are several common ways by which churches make planning decisions. Sometimes it is by delusion, that is, by acting on assumptions that are no longer true—sentimentality, nostalgia, emotional ties to the past, the "way it used to be." To make decisions about the future based on what was true years ago, or what we hope will be valid again, is to delude ourselves. This procedure will attract only those with the same mind-set. It will not work for long, if at all. If the church is to be more than an ingrown, historical society, it must minister to the true needs of people living in the present, real world.

Another planning method is that of decree, which is similar to dictatorship. A strong, vocal pastor or layperson overpowers others and literally dictates the "solution." Occasionally, the individual speaks very little, but that person's money shouts aloud. The threat of major financial withdrawal (or support) can coerce a congregation into action that would not occur with the use of normal, participative processes. Church leaders should be aware of this possibility, and they should make it known from the very beginning that the standard voting procedures of their constitution will be followed.

Planning decisions can also be handled by a process which actually amounts to default. This includes a variety of steps which move responsibility from one board to another, postponing action ad infinitum in the hope that the problem will go away. It never does, however, and in the meantime the problem becomes more serious and opportunities for ministry are lost. Perhaps one of the more important skills requiring development in the future is that prophetic ability to identify and acknowledge holes in the dike before they become torrential floods.

When a church reacts to crisis, or attempts to decide by delusion, decree, or default, it most often wanders aimlessly. The price for doing this is always high. There is an emotional price as members fail to find common direction for their efforts. If there is not even agreement on a variety of diverse program goals, fragmentation often results. There is also a material price to pay when serious planning is omitted.

A church in the West constructed a small, first-unit building without giving adequate thought to the future. The city council was petitioned to open a new street giving access to the church building. The congregation paid for the installation of that new street. In only a few years, the church grew rapidly under the leadership of a popular, skilled pastor. A decision was made to expand the building. Instead of going out of state to an architect with a "stock plan" as was done previously, local professionals were engaged this time. It was soon .discovered that the first unit was located on the site in such a way that it could not be expanded in any direction. The city council was approached once more, this time with a petition to close the same street! The street was purchased back from the city and removed, again at the church's expense, and a new facility added where the street had been. The long-term time and expense was much higher than it would have been if adequate planning had been accomplished in the first place.

Why should churches plan for the future? Because planning is consistent with biblical theology; it is the best way to meet accelerating change; it allows us to form the future rather than to react to emergencies; it permits intentional action rather than decisions by delusion, decree, or default; it costs less, emotionally and materially, in the long run.

How to Plan

Much has been written on the subject of the planning process. Strategic planning is now relatively common for organizations of all types. There are many models to follow. The procedure contained herein has been used for over nine years. It has been monitored from start to finish with dozens of churches from at least eight different denominations. It is a process that requires a review of all church programs with involvement in the process by the entire congregation. Furthermore, while not prejudicial toward the need for building improvements, this approach does seriously take this possibility into account and provides options should they be required.

Essentially, strategic planning means moving from the general to the specific; from the basic concerns to the details of proposed solutions; from goals and objectives to strategies, tactics, and action steps. The process usually moves on, full-cycle, into evaluation, then back to a review of the objectives based on experience.

When thinking of the future, often the first tendency is to be overconcerned about details. Perhaps there is a similarity here to the way physical illness is handled. The symptoms appear first. They may be rather minor, but irritating. Relief is sought from the symptoms. However, a good physician will probe beyond these to the source. The symptoms come from the disease, not the reverse. When the disease is diagnosed and cured, the symptoms disappear.

Everything a congregation does springs from the source, the center, which is the common perception of its mission in the world, its reason for being. When there is acceptance of that basic purpose, other questions can be asked and answered. Exactly how, when, and where does the church carry out its mission? What organizational procedure will be used and who will guide it? What facilities and budget will be required? There must be agreement on the central concerns before answers can be found for each succeeding stage of detailed questions.

All of this does not say that any answers will be automatic. Much work is still involved, but the effort becomes exciting because there is a central, common focus. New challenges will constantly arise, and yet the struggle will be within the context of a deliberate movement in a chosen direction. Without agreement on the central concerns, there is often a sense of isolation or of fighting against the tide. As in all navigation toward a destination, the course must be checked periodically. In most churches, a review of the basic mission is essential every three to five years. When affirmation is received on this basis, members can move to their specific, week-by-week ministries with confidence.

At this point, it should be said that careful planning builds on what has happened previously without forgetting the past, enshrining it, or being defensive about it. The church is an ongoing, living body. Some of its efforts have been very worthwhile, others less so. Improvement is always possible. To plan wisely is to affirm the worthwhile programs, expand on them, and remove as much as possible of that which is underproductive.

The foregoing philosophy has serious implications regarding both time scheduling and organization. When a congregation decides to begin a long-range planning process, sufficient time must be allowed to give everyone an opportunity to participate in defining the basic goals of the church. At first glance, these goals might appear to be self-evident and the same for every church. Experience usually proves otherwise, especially when it comes to defining exactly what the goal means for the congregation and how it is to be carried out. There must be a considerable amount of communication to reach agreement on a clear definition of basic goals and to achieve widespread understanding. This process takes at least two months for a small church of one hundred members and between three and six months for larger congregations. An additional three to six months is required to move into more specific proposals regarding program strategies, to prioritize these in the context of the human and material resources available, and to consider the future implications for staff, budget, and facilities.

The Planning Process

The planning process requires four or five task groups (or working committees) with members chosen according to their interest and ability in that particular task. An additional criteria for selecting leadership is that all elements of congregational life be represented, such as those from various theological viewpoints, age groups, classes, and interests. A Data-Gathering Task Group provides the factual information necessary for wise decision making. A Program-Goal Task Group works with the congregation in establishing goals and the methods by which they may be implemented. A Communications Task Group is responsible for that two-way movement of information which is so essential for a fruitful planning effort. A Financial Task Group evaluates the material resources of the church. At a later time, if it is necessary, a Building Task Group handles the details of construction. All task group members together form the Planning Council.

The number of people involved will vary with the membership of the congregation. Another factor is the optimum size for a task group to accomplish its work effectively. The minimum number for each group would be three persons. A typical size is five to eight persons. Efficiency seems best when no more than eleven persons are on a Task Group. The largest number is usually required by the Program-Goal Task Group.

The normal flow of responsibility, recommendations, and decision making is from the Task Group to the Planning Council and then to the congregation. When a group, such as Data-Gathering, finishes its specific task, the members still serve on the Planning Council. When groups exist for only part of the planning process, it is tempting to blame others for any problems. There is also an advantage in having the various elements of the congregation represented throughout. Furthermore, if some planning goals are rejected, the groups are accountable to recommend other options. Finally, this type of organization is geared to review comprehensively all of the interrelated programs and resources of the church. This is certainly only one of several organizational types that provide the key elements of continuity, representation, comprehensiveness, and accountability.

Establishing the Data Base

Any planning is only as good as the facts on which it is based. When congregational members look to the future, they need to know the facts and trends of the past and present. In retail trade, there are those who plan their purchases and others who are impulse buyers. The impulse buyer often regrets the purchase the next day when the impulse is gone and also tends to have difficulty making payments. Without widespread dissemination of the necessary facts, church members tend to vote their emotions. Here, too, there is usually the problem of "the morning after."

Accurate and complete data provide a broad base of self-understanding from which will spring the actions of the other Task Groups. Facts are needed about church membership, attendance, finances, staff, programs, and facilities. In addition, information is required regarding the community where the church is located. No congregation ministers in isolation. Trends in population, housing, employment, land use, economics, transportation, and related areas are essential as well as data about other churches and agencies that serve people. Also, the projections of municipal planning agencies can be most helpful. The church must know the community needs and opportunities if it is to serve effectively. About three months is usually needed to gather the basic information. (See Appendix A for suggested church and community data outline.)

The data base should be compiled by the Task Group in such a way that it may be clearly understood by the congregation. This implies using visuals, such as charts and graphs, rather than masses of numerical statistics. Furthermore, the facts should be available for study by each member over a reasonable period of time. Normally, this means provision of a data booklet for each member-family rather than (or in addition to) a group presentation which may not leave a long-lasting impression. The importance of a substantial data base for good planning cannot be overemphasized. These facts should be available before various options are defined and evaluated.

A large midwestern congregation appointed a Building Committee with only the thought in mind of replacing its somewhat dilapidated worship area. Thorough research was desired, however, and the Data-Gathering Committee brought in some information that shattered earlier assumptions. Based on these facts, major questions were raised about the adequacy of the site in terms of size and location related to projected future programming. Eventually, the vast majority of the congregation voted to sell and relocate. Today, the greatly expanded ministry of that church can be traced directly to its willingness to gather essential data and take seriously what it had to say. A substantial data base is a prerequisite to good planning.

Developing Program Goals

To define the primary mission of the church and establish goals for its implementation requires members to be open to new perceptions and to the thoughts of others. Synonymous with this attitude of openness is the spirit of humility which admits: "I do not know everything. I want to learn and hear the opinions of others before reaching definite conclusions."

Consider the poem by John Godfrey Saxe, "The Blind Men and the Elephant," in which he describes a group of blind men who were placed near an elephant. They were told to touch the elephant and say what they thought it was. Each blind man touched a part of the animal nearest to him, and from that he conceived his image of the whole. Thus, the side of the elephant felt like a wall, the tusk a spear, the trunk a snake, the knee a tree, the ear a fan, and the tail a rope. The poet concluded:

> "And so these men of Indostan
> Disputed loud and long,
> Each in his own opinion
> Exceeding stiff and strong,
> Though each was partly in the right,
> And all were in the wrong!"[1]

Groups within the church can be very much like these blind men of Indostan. If each member is responsive only in terms of her or his own experiences and perceptions, no matter how valid they may be, the composite view will likely be very distorted. The goals of any church will be greatly limited if determined by persons whose concepts of reality and meanings of faith issue solely out of their own understanding. For the total view, members need each other. Much

---

[1] *A Treasury of the Familiar,* edited by Ralph L. Woods (New York: The Macmillan Company, 1946), p. 8. Permission to quote received from Houghton Mifflin Company, Boston, Mass.

work is involved, but the quality of the result justifies the time and effort expended.

The purpose of the research involved in fact gathering and goal setting is to expand the vision, to draw upon the knowledge and experience of others, to stretch the imagination, and to increase awareness of the available options. Unlike the blind men of Indostan, serious planners need to comprehend the whole picture.

The work of the Program-Goal Task Group begins simultaneously with that of the Data-Gathering Group. If they are to lead the congregation in an objective review of the best options, the Program-Goal Group members must demonstrate openness of attitude by their own example. Perhaps the first session of this group should be a funeral celebration, burying any and all preconceived solutions. Most people find it very difficult to assess any long-standing habit or opinion from a different perspective. People are creatures of habit and enjoy the security of the known. However, most giant steps of progress in human history have come only when there was a sincere willingness to take a new look at the old and familiar.

Imagine life today if some ancient ancestor had decided not to approach again the problem of transporting goods from one place to another, and had been satisfied with the cargo sled drawn by animals or persons. A fresh perspective toward transportation needs resulted in the invention of that essential but taken-for-granted product, the wheel. Imagine the contrast in contemporary life if Edison had been satisfied with candles or kerosine to meet lighting needs, instead of taking the persistent and creative approach which led to the invention of the electric light bulb.

In recent years, a fountain-pen company felt that although seemingly everything possible had been done to improve their product, there was still a market for a better writing device. In a brainstorming session the company's engineers were urged to describe in elementary terms the goal of the pen company. Finally the team described their product in two words. The goal of the company was to produce devices that "make marks." With this freeing definition, the engineers forgot about fountain pens, went back to their laboratories, and developed the now universal ballpoint pen!

Congregations today need to take a new look at their basic principles of mission in ways unhampered by the easy but increasingly inadequate answers of the past. Church members need that simple yet profound freeing definition of congregational goals which will allow the emergence of new and better methods of achieving those goals. Many excellent ideas regarding programs, stewardship, and the use of facilities fall on deaf ears because they are new, different, or are thought to be somewhat risky. But the wheel, the electric light bulb, the ballpoint pen, and the extremely effective church never arise from a defensive, status-quo, stifling atmosphere.

To expand their minds, the members of the Program-Goal Task Group should begin with wide reading of books and articles that tell about the creative and helpful ministries of other churches. Because the experience of individuals is limited, they turn to others. Knowledge of their struggles, successes, and failures is essential to serious planning. Direct contact with leaders from churches in the community or while traveling can augment this research in a personal way.

In the very beginning, the group may feel that there are only a few realistic options. After two or three months of reading, visiting, and group discussion, the perception may change to thinking that there are dozens of them! If so, it should be realized that the total congregation can probably deal with no more than six options at one time in any depth. Thus, after full discussion, priorities need to be assigned so that the choices may be limited to a reasonable number.

Another topic that requires early attention by members of the Program-Goal Task Group is their perception of the congregational level of understanding concerning the planning effort. Some members may think that there are only two or three specific problems needing attention and will want to concentrate on those apart from comprehensive planning. If serious planning has been done in the recent past, decisions can certainly be made based on the criteria and priorities of that planning. But if this is not the case, then what appear to be minor problems can have a major effect because of the interrelatedness of each part of that living body, the church. When one board decides to allocate money, time, and/or personnel to a specific need, there are less of those key resources available for other needs.

As an example, there is now a long-term energy shortage almost everywhere. The utilities bills of some churches have already increased so much that the number of paid, professional staff has had to be reduced. With this a present and coming trend, how will churches plan? The starting point is to recognize that a concern in one area always affects other areas and, thus, decisions made independently without considering the ramifications elsewhere are always poor decisions. The Program-Goal Task Group, therefore, has a responsibility to raise the level of consciousness of the congregation to the need for total, comprehensive planning that relates all programs, budget, staff, boards, and related factors to their basic mission.

As the totality of the church passes in review, three questions should be asked.

1. Related to the basic mission of this church, what of that which is now being accomplished is of high enough priority to be retained, and how can modifications be made for greater effectiveness?

2. Related to the basic mission of this church, what of that which is presently being accomplished is of low priority so that the resources it requires could be used to meet higher priorities?

3. What new ministries should be started to accomplish more fully the basic mission of this church?

Essential to serious planning is the willingness to add, eliminate, or modify present programs so that all efforts are seen as coordinated to help fulfill the basic goals of the church.

To be effective, a broad review of total church life must offer the opportunity for involvement of the entire membership. Not all will respond, of course, but the possibility should be available. Furthermore, it is best to provide more than one time and method of participation. Many members who will not speak out in a large, open meeting will give valuable ideas in a small group of eight to twelve people. Others who do not verbalize their thoughts well may respond to an Opinion Finder Questionnaire. At least these three methods should be used for maximum participation. Involvement enhances communication and assures a high percentage of ownership of proposed goals.

The timing for broad congregational participation comes after three major tasks have been accomplished. First, the Data-Gathering Group should have its factual report compiled and distributed to all member-families in time for it to have been read, understood, and the trends reviewed. Second, the Program-Goal Group will have completed its research and identified several major, realistic options for future ministry. (While it is important to limit the options, the group should also be open to other options that might surface later.) These options will be defined and their implications outlined in enough detail for productive discussion. Third, the Program-Goal Group will also have interviewed the staff, officers, boards, and key committees of the church to learn their evaluation of present programs and hopes for the future.

Seeking Congregational Participation

With this kind of background, the congregation is ready for its informed input. Some general principles to share with the members at this time include the following:

1. Be open to new and different possibilities. Be objective in making judgments. Consider questions from more than one perspective.

2. Look to the future rather than to the past. What can happen in the future is most important. Do not let history be an anchor.

3. Think logically as well as theologically. Apply the same, rational thinking tools to the church as is done when planning on the job or at home. In thinking, move from the general to the specific.

4. Love those who have different opinions. Listen to what the other person says as carefully as you expect others to listen to you. Reach for consensus rather than conflict or compromise. Seek unity on priorities that are consistent with Scripture.

5. Be patient. Do not expect immediate solutions for problems that have been present for years. Establish a realistic schedule allowing sufficient time for research, full congregational involvement, and wide communication.

As the preceding list indicates, the first principle for congregational participation is the willingness of members to try to "step outside themselves" to assess more objectively their situation. A downtown church in a small eastern city owned a fine building but found attendance and membership decreasing and average age of members increasing. Members were continuing a ministry which was becoming more irrelevant to their changing environment each year. Consultants met with church leaders and listed a number of reasons for choosing a church home. Group members were asked to imagine themselves as 30-year-old parents who had just moved into the community. Which criteria would be most important to them in selecting a church home? Their list included:

1) Good Christian education program for children and young couples
2) Convenient location
3) Adequate parking
4) Friendly people of similar age
5) Outstanding preaching
6) Impressive sanctuary
7) Excellent music program
8) Proud history
9) Opportunities to serve community
10) Leadership opportunities
11) Bible study groups
12) Small sharing groups
13) Fellowship and recreation programs
14) A variety of programs from which to choose
15) Celebration/involvement type of worship

When the results were tallied, the top five criteria were compared with the current strengths of the church. Major differences were noted between what the church offered and what such community newcomers would probably desire. Since the leaders themselves had rated the criteria, they subsequently felt more ownership of the discovered needs and were more willing to plan necessary changes. This or some similar procedure will help members to face the needs honestly.

Congregational involvement is also needed to place the major options in priority order. When sufficient time is given to thinking about it, most churches become quite enthusiastic about doing more work than their human and material resources will allow. While this attitude is healthy, it must be tempered with the realization that a focusing of resources usually brings better results than being spread too thin. Also, a fair balance should be sought between programs aimed primarily at the membership and those which reach out to the community, the nation, and the world.

Complications usually arise in the prioritizing process. One major concern is often the condition or location of the church building. While this subject cannot be ignored, too often it becomes the determining factor. Viewed in its proper perspective, the church building is a tool to aid the congregation in fulfilling its mission. Churches can minister without buildings. In fact, they have, and some do today. The building as a tool can either limit or support the church in fulfilling its mission. This is the perspective from which judgments about buildings ought to be made. Part of the confusion arises from the very usage of that word "church." The church is the Body of Christ, the people of God, the fellowship of believers. The building that is sometimes used should never be called the church.

The least that can be done is to refer to it as "church house" or "church building" or "meeting place." It would be best to create an entirely new word for the physical plant used by the congregation, but until the time when (and if) that happens, the examples set by a few wise churches could be followed. On the sign out front, change "Trinity Church" to "Trinity Church meets here" or "Trinity Church worships here." This could be the beginning point in reeducation on this subject.

While most people would agree that far too many resources go into the construction and maintenance of buildings, the non-building church movement has not moved very far. Perhaps in America the reason is an obsession with materialism or an exaggerated "sense of place" that borders on idolatry. At any rate, for too long now the tail has wagged the dog as buildings have determined what the church is and does. When 50 percent or more of the budget goes into mortgage payments, interest, utilities, and maintenance, the church becomes servant to its building. When neighborhood children are barred because they might mark the fellowship room walls, the building begins to dictate the ministry. When needed new staff or programs cannot be added because there is still a twelve-year mortgage on space that is used one hour a week, the building has set, in concrete, the priorities of the church. When programs are confined to one neighborhood, the building has made ministry inflexible, if not ineffective.

As various options are seriously considered, the building's role must be carefully evaluated. If planners understand the meaning and purpose of the church, they will not allow the physical plant to have undue influence in the prioritizing process.

Preparing Recommendations

When, through the sharing of information and a high degree of involvement, the congregation has chosen its top priorities for future ministry, the next step is for the Program-Goal Task Group to prepare recommendations that have a reasonable chance of being implemented. Some criteria to be considered include:

1. The recommendations should cover every aspect of the life of the church. In viewing their work together, most congregations will have both "generalist" and "specialist" roles. There will be a group of programs considered normal for most churches plus a few special ministries based upon the unique neighborhood nearby, or predominant age group, or particular talents and interest of the members. Noted church planner Lyle Schaller recommends that there is strength and focus in a church having one or two specialties in addition to fulfilling the "generalist" role.[2] Regardless of which role it is, recommendations usually fit under one of the following categories:

(*a*) Worship. Included are such topics as preaching, music, drama, Communion, baptism, ushering, weddings, funerals, midweek meetings, and special services.

(*b*) Education. This covers all ages and includes church school, youth groups, curriculum, camps, retreats, home and family education, leadership training, and special seminars.

(*c*) Outreach. Included are visitation and all types of evangelism, social services, retirement homes, hospitals, home and international missions, persons of special need, etc.

(*d*) Fellowship. This includes both formal and informal fellowship events, dinners, recreation, receptions, crafts, and hobbies.

(*e*) Administration. Included are the church constitution and record keeping, organizational plan, professional staff, publicity, finances, and long-range planning.

2. The recommendations should be written in very specific language. Rather than "we recommend increased efforts to minister to young adults," it is better to say "we recommend that a new church school class be started by the Board of Christian Education within three months for those twenty to thirty years of age; that a fellowship dinner be held for this age group every second month starting in September; that a list be compiled by July 15 of young adults who have attended services and that all of them be visited by the deacons within one month." Unless a recommendation is quite specific, the chances of implementation are low.

[2] Lyle E. Schaller, *Hey, That's Our Church!* (Nashville: Abingdon Press, 1975), pp. 137-141; used with permission.

3. The recommendations should include as many procedures as possible for their implementation. It is best not to assume too much. Indicate not only what is to be done but also how to do it.

4. The recommendations should include a clear assignment of responsibility. Designated to oversee the work could be a board, committee, special task group, individual church officer, or staff person. Definite accountability is essential.

5. The recommendations should include some means of measurement, either numerically or within a time-frame (or both). Without having a definite goal toward which to work, there would be no way to evaluate progress. Furthermore, if there is no particular time by which the program or elements of it are to be completed, procrastination tends to occur. The timing and responsibility for future evaluation should also be included.

6. The recommendations should include what their implications are for budget, personnel (staff and members), and facilities. This is when the question of realism must be faced squarely. It is a healthy experience to think about what the church could be and do if it had unlimited resources. To aim high is to achieve more. Such dreams and hopes lift Christians to loftier levels of committed stewardship. However, even the greatest degree of congregational commitment must be honestly measured against the program goals and priorities to determine what is achievable now and what must await future fulfillment. To challenge high commitment with impossible goals is to invite frustration and despair. If the recommendation requires space or personnel or budget clearly beyond the capacity of the church, it has failed to meet this criterion. As has been considered previously, enthusiastic involvement of the membership in a serious planning process often brings forth more ideas for ministry than can be achieved in a hundred years. When handled wisely, this abundance is good! To handle wisely means that goals are assigned a priority related to the overall mission of the church and that those of lower priority will be accomplished as soon as the necessary resources are available.

7. The recommendations should include a priority listing, both within each major section and at the conclusion. Within the category of education, for example, will be listed those top priority recommendations which are considered essential in helping to fulfill the overall mission of the church and are also crucial in terms of timing because there are current, urgent needs affecting a significant

percentage of the church's constituency. Other recommendations will be given lower priority because they are considered not as closely related to the mission; they affect the lives of fewer people, or they are not as urgently required at this point in time. After priorities are established within each major program category of the church, it will probably be necessary for the planning leaders to recommend an overall priority listing to the congregation. This will foster the health of the total church body. There is no advantage of possessing a tremendously muscular arm if the heart is about to give out. A balance is needed among program elements if the church is to minister effectively to the whole person and if it is to appeal to the broad, diverse spectrum of contemporary society.

Adopting Recommendations

After carefully preparing recommendations according to criteria such as these, the Program-Goal Task Group will want to present them to the congregation for consideration. The most complete deliberation can be given to those recommendations which are distributed in written form at least two weeks prior to the meeting in which they are voted upon. This allows time for comprehension, discussion, and questions. As is true throughout any serious planning effort, the Communications Task Group will be sharing much information using a variety of media concerning the process of decision making, the rationale supporting the recommendations, and details regarding the congregational business meeting.

If there has been thorough research, a high degree of membership involvement, and adequate communication, the recommendations probably will be adopted. Churches following these procedures have averaged better than an 80 percent affirmative vote on their planning recommendations. This has been true even when the recommendations involved major changes in programming, facilities, or location for ministry. Experience indicates that at least a two-thirds majority vote is needed to implement successfully such major changes. It is most helpful to make this majority a requirement of the vote.

There are many other types of planning[3] and nonplanning. The process described herein requires considerable effort, some monetary outlay, and up to a full year of time. The results are worth it.

[3] A helpful resource is *Local Church Planning Manual,* by Richard K. Gladden, Norman M. Green, and Richard E. Rusbuldt (Valley Forge: Judson Press, 1977).

Six Planning Options for Churches 2

As information is gathered and discussion held regarding the planning options being considered, the top three to six possibilities need to be ranked in order of priority. As has previously been pointed out, the role of the church building should not have an unproportionate influence over decision making, but it is too vital a factor to be ignored. The building and its cost, both initially and in terms of upkeep, often are the major hindrances to any reallocation of resources to programs aimed at meeting the needs of people.

Thus, it seems appropriate to share information about six specific planning options that many congregations may seriously consider as they honestly face all the implications of being good stewards of their resources. Program and facility planning are both essentially intertwined in each of these options.

The Multi-Church Location

Today, the typical church building is utilized very few hours each week. Even if there are programs in some spaces, such as a Child Development (Day Care) Center using several classrooms, recreational space, and the kitchen, large areas such as that used for worship stand empty. This type of poor stewardship will not be possible for most congregations much longer because of the increasing cost of construction, utilities, and maintenance. Thus, a very realistic alternative is to share facilities with one or more other congregations.

As the song puts it, "Everything Old Is New Again." The concept of shared facilities is not a revolutionary new idea. However, like the rediscovery of solar energy, perhaps the events of history have now emerged in such a way that the time has come for wider consideration of sharing.

The argument could possibly be made that the church of the New Testament era worshiped in a shared facility since those Christians utilized the Jewish synagogue for their first services. There are many examples of this concept in nineteenth-century America. During the first half of that century, in the state of New York, "as often as not, the first church building in a town was erected by general subscription and shared on alternate Sundays by at least two sects."[1]

In Pennsylvania, starting around 1817, there was often "a co-operative affiliation in the local community between the Lutheran and Reformed congregations, who owned and used a common church property and the building, where they worshipped on alternate Sundays. The degree of co-operation ranged from joint ownership of the property, with separate services, consistories [places of assembly] and Sunday Schools, to churches with a common consistory, Sunday School, treasury, and even union services. Hundreds of these union or community churches were founded until about 1900. . . ."[2] The shared facility concept must be distinguished from a merger or a federation. When two (or more) churches merge, they become one in organizational polity, in pastoral leadership, in denominational affiliation, in holding services, in budgeting, in everything. When churches federate, they unite for services, programs, use of facilities and pastoral leadership, but they usually retain separate denominational connections, membership rolls, budgets, organizations, mission giving, etc. Often it is required that the pastoral leadership rotate regularly among the denominations involved.

The sharing of a building is a much different concept. Each participating congregation retains its own denominational affiliation with all of the theological implications that involves. Each group is totally autonomous and independent. Each church has its own pastor, constitution, officers, and budget. Each congregation holds its own services. The only ingredients that need to be shared to make this concept work are the physical plant and, preferably, the

[1]Whitney R. Cross, *The Burned-Over District* (Ithaca, N.Y.: Cornell University Press, 1950), p. 42.
[2]Ruth Rouse and Stephen C. Neill, eds., *A History of the Ecumenical Movement, 1517–1948* (Philadelphia: The Westminster Press, 1954), p. 242.

ownership and management of property which is shared.

The sharing of a building by two or more churches is an eminently practical idea. Because of their large assembly rooms, ecclesiastical structures usually require long, heavy, supporting beams and high ceilings, both of which add to initial expense. Large, high spaces are difficult and costly to heat and cool. Construction, maintenance, and utilities costs decrease greatly in a shared building. There is thus maximum stewardship of resources.

Another reason to consider sharing is because it is a very efficient option. Every church has many program needs as they attempt to fulfill their ministry. Increasingly, congregations find that they cannot afford to provide good facilities for all of their programs. When there is sharing, each congregation has access to space beyond what they can afford alone. Duplication is eliminated as the rooms complement each other. The smallest church can use the assembly area of its larger co-inhabitant for that occasional big wedding, funeral, or special service. Likewise, the larger church can use the fellowship or worship space of its smaller sister for programs that require a more intimate setting. This is enhanced, of course, if all the available spaces are flexible and multipurpose. Even if they are not, shared spaces are still more efficient than a building that is used by one congregation only.

Why share facilities? Webster has defined a word which perhaps best sums it up: "Synergism—cooperative action of discrete agencies such that the total effect is greater than the sum of the effects taken independently." Congregations now sharing facilities feel that their action is synergistic in nature. The programs that they can implement and the space available are more than the total possible from two or three individual congregations.

Successful sharing of facilities has occurred in recent years in such places as Canada and England as well as the United States. Examples include: Lander, Wyoming (Lutheran and Disciples); Caldwell, Idaho (Lutheran and Disciples); Kansas City, Missouri (Episcopal, United Church of Christ, Presbyterian, and Catholic); Kansas City, Kansas (Methodist and Mennonite); Sacramento, California (Baptist and Brethren); Wilton, Connecticut (Presbyterian and Episcopal); Portland, Oregon (United Church of Christ, Presbyterian, Baptists, and Disciples); Washington, D.C. (Hebrew and Episcopal); and Mankato, Minnesota (Methodist, Baptist, and United Church of Christ).

Although this idea sounds very logical and practical, it must be recognized that sharing a building is a little like living in a commune with other families. There must be very solid agreement at the beginning and very clear communication on a regular basis if it is going to work. The subjects that require complete understanding include:

1. The basic reasons for wanting to share space. All the motivating factors, including survival, economics, cooperation, and theology, must be honestly presented and openly discussed. Each congregation needs to know why the other is there if a wise decision is to be made that minimizes the potential for future misunderstandings.

2. The study process that will lead to a decision. It is best if this is accomplished jointly with committees composed of members from each interested congregation. The full involvement of many lay leaders is essential. While clergy support is important, there is nothing that can substitute for grassroots membership involvement and enthusiasm. Sufficient time is required for gathering facts, reviewing them, establishing goals, and determining if these goals can be accomplished better through the use of a shared facility. Normally, at least one year of research is required for the kind of understanding that leads to an informed decision, and additional time may be necessary if more than two churches are involved. A qualified, objective consultant can add immeasurably to the success of the study process.

3. Procedures for decision making. At the conclusion of the study process, written proposals are presented to each congregation and votes are received simultaneously. Prior agreement is necessary on the percentage of vote required for affirmation. Facility sharing is not advisable if based on a simple majority vote. Approval by at least 65 percent and up to 80 percent or more of the members will markedly increase the chances for successful implementation.

4. Location of property. Even for a single congregational body, decisions about buildings and property can be traumatic because of the many emotional ties that are present. Naturally, the trauma increases when two or more churches are involved. Therefore, this decision, above all, must be based upon fully documented facts. Factors include proximity to the members,

parking available, neighborhood characteristics, other nearby churches, growth potential, accessibility, site advantages, and disposition of present properties. An agreement to share implies the willingness to seek that location which will best serve each congregation in the future, even if it is not the property currently owned by any church.

5. Ownership of buildings and property. Portions of some shared facilities are totally owned by the participating congregations in a condominium-style arrangement. As an example, one church using this procedure owns the worship space and the land on which it is constructed, while the other congregation owns the educational and fellowship space. The buildings are connected and each church is relying on using the space of the other for the operation of its total program. A written agreement states the procedures for this relationship.

   Probably a superior way is participation in a Religious Facilities Corporation which owns the buildings and property. Depending upon its size and financial strength, each church then has part-ownership of the total facility. This avoids the potential "yours" and "mine" argument since everything is "ours." Carefully prepared legal documents spell out such important details as arrangements for payment of utilities and maintenance expenses, the mortgage retirement plan, how remodeling and building additions are to be handled, procedures for terminating the arrangement or adding other congregations, ownership of furnishings and equipment, changes necessitated by increasing or decreasing membership, and use of the building.

6. Scheduling the use of space. Central scheduling should be accomplished far in advance of need. If this is done, conflict will be avoided. Most church programs have sufficient flexibility that minor adjustment can be made providing that those involved are aware well ahead of time. Experience has demonstrated that it all works well if a Christian attitude is taken toward the needs of others. When compared with the cost savings and other advantages offered by shared facilities, a few occasional scheduling inconveniences are a very small price to pay.

7. Program and staff cooperation. Sharing space makes it more convenient to build upon and complement the strengths of each

congregation. Some churches share office space, equipment, and secretarial service, thereby realizing economies and increased efficiency. When willing to do so, professional staff can draw upon the special talents of each other and substitute during illness, vacation, or when there is a pastoral vacancy. The combined group can share programs when it is advantageous to all, for example, in the youth area, or unite to engage speakers, drama, or musical programs which would be difficult or impossible for one congregation to support by itself. If the members and staff are willing to combine their efforts, the possibilities for program sharing are many.

The accompanying illustration shows the arrangement used in the "Multi-Church Center" in Mankato, Minnesota, by Methodist, Congregational/United Church of Christ, and Baptist congregations. A fellowship-dining-overflow space separates two worship

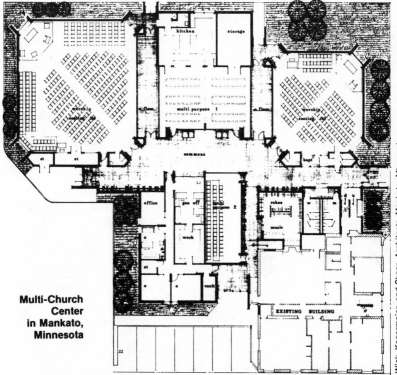

Multi-Church Center in Mankato, Minnesota

Wick, Kagermeier, and Skaar, Architects, Mankato, Minnesota

areas. Good acoustical, folding doors allow complete opening of the total area to seat approximately one thousand people, division into four separate spaces with two hallways, or any combination in between. A flat floor and flexible seating are required for this arrangement.

The Mankato leaders have experienced the many program and stewardship advantages of this plan. Four services are held each Sunday in the two worship spaces. An existing educational building was remodeled for use by all three churches. By voluntary decision, there is sharing in the church school, youth work, and office arrangements. Joint programs are held periodically. Both clergy and lay leaders are extremely pleased with the functioning of their shared facility.

The construction of a new building is best accomplished when the architects' design flows from the program goals of the churches involved. New construction makes it somewhat easier to achieve a satisfactory result in sharing space. However, sharing can still occur in an existing building if some remodeling is possible and if there is a willingness to live with the problems (usually minor) of a structure that was originally designed for one congregation. Obviously, all of the advantages, disadvantages, and cost factors must be carefully evaluated in reaching a decision. The multi-church location is definitely an option worthy of serious consideration.[3]

The Multi-Location Church

After just reviewing the advantages of sharing space, it may seem inappropriate to consider the church which uses more than one location and building. How could this planning option possibly be responsible stewardship of resources? Perhaps a brief review of the history of many large, inner-city American churches will help to shed some light on this legitimate question.

Between ten and thirty years ago, such a church had over one thousand members and an outstanding preacher who attracted people from the entire metropolitan area. It was the leading church of its denomination in the city. The choir was excellent. Numerous community and interchurch cultural events were held in the spacious auditorium. The large church plant was worth in excess of $1 million.

[3]For further details on this option, see Ralph L. Belknap and Richard L. Critz, *Shared Facilities: the Mankato Center* (King of Prussia, Pa.: Religious Publishing Co., 1977).

Then, rather suddenly it seemed, the character of the neighborhood began to change. Membership, attendance, and giving fell steadily while utilities and maintenance costs of the building increased. Members moved farther away, and it became more difficult for them to drive to meetings, especially during the week. While some members wanted to minister more actively to their new neighbors, most were not interested. The building was vandalized almost weekly. The church could no longer afford to pay a great preacher, choir director, and organist. Finally, a meeting of key leaders was held to determine what to do.

Does this sound familiar? At this point, the story could move in one of several directions. The church could relocate to the suburbs. By using endowment funds, it could hang on where it is for a few added years. It could try ministering more seriously to its neighborhood with the relatively few members willing to do that. Merger is another possibility, or it could disband. The years during which the building is greatly underutilized are years of very poor stewardship. Forced sale usually results in a major financial loss. More importantly, it is both sad and unproductive for the kingdom of God to have a strong, living church degenerate into ineffectiveness.

A scattered few congregations across the country have decided that it is better stewardship in the long run to carry out their ministry in two (or more) locations. In several cases, this has allowed a strong church to remain strong. One absolute essential for a multi-location church is that this decision be made soon enough that the option is chosen from a position of strength. While it is impossible to give precise statistics regarding the strength required, one general measure could be that the church have membership size and budget support sufficient to employ at least two fully trained, full-time professional staff members. Even so, there are successful exceptions to this criteria.

The major advantages of the multi-location church are that a wide variety of programs may be offered and that there is a reasonable chance of retaining a strong financial base. The First Baptist Church of Kansas City, Missouri, is a representative example of both advantages. This congregation has now moved into its second multi-location ministry! Actually, this is not a unique or new pattern. It was common on the frontier for a church to have "branches" or to hold services in more than one community. *The Memoir of John Mason Peck* states that in 1838 "he was with unanimity elected to the pastorship of the Baptist Church worshipping at Rock Spring and Zoar." This is also a strong tradition with the Church of the Brethren. There are several examples today in Lancaster County, Pennsylvania.

In 1909 the Kansas City Church sold its old building and moved to a new location on Linwood Boulevard, then at the center of the city's residential growth. At the same time, the church built a West Side Branch to serve the downtown area. That building was sold to the Salvation Army in the early 1940s. Then, as the city expanded and the Linwood neighborhood changed, another location was established in 1961. This is in the suburban community of Red Bridge, twelve miles away from the Linwood building.

The downtown ministry centers on the nearby residents and includes a very active program with the aged. A major section of the building was leased for six years to a Comprehensive Health Center which provided much needed services to the neighborhood. Between 250 and 300 persons per day were served by a staff of nearly 100. Regardless of where they live, First Baptist members can participate in the unique ministries required in the downtown Linwood area.

The Red Bridge location offers the more "traditional" programs of a suburban, family-centered congregation. People are given a wide variety of choices for the use of their time and talents. In addition, the suburban ministry attracts many who would not go downtown for their church affiliation. This helps to assure the necessary financial base for operating effectively at both locations. Thus, the multi-location church does have stewardship advantages in the management of resources.

This type of congregation is one church in every significant aspect. There is one membership roll, one constitution, one set of officers. One professional staff serves both locations. Often the service hours are arranged so that the senior minister preaches in both locations each Sunday, but the staff can develop a team ministry so that this is not necessary. Usually, the location for meetings, dinners, and other all-congregational events is rotated between the separate buildings. In connection with the previous option, there is no reason why the space at one or both locations cannot be shared with another church should that prove possible and mutually advantageous. As a matter of fact, another congregation is now sharing the Linwood building in Kansas City. For the large, downtown church in a changing neighborhood, two locations could well be an option.

The Kansas City senior minister, the Reverend Malcolm E. Haughey, gives the reasons supporting this option: "We serve more people than either building could serve alone. We have at least the potential for a richer church life, more responsive to total community needs, than we would if we were simply in either of our two communities. We are seeking to develop not simply a one-pastor centered ministry but a team ministry to help the whole congregation take part in the ministry as the people of God. Specifically, our two-building ministry has enabled us to do a number of things.

(1) It has enabled a church caught in rapid change and facing an unknown future to take positive steps to serve its scattered membership and preserve the continuity of its history in service to the community and world.

(2) It enabled the church to begin a stronger suburban ministry than would have been possible with a church extension project.

(3) It enabled the church to remain in the inner city, providing a church home for a large number of people still living in the area and for others for whom the building there is still central. At the same time, it gave the congregation an opportunity to work in helping meet community needs.

(4) It has enabled staff and members to be involved in creative ministry across suburban and inner city lines. For example, a task force made up, in part, by those who worship in the suburban church, has been working with a Thursday evening program with several hundred black teenagers. Another task force, made up of women who live in apartments and worship in the central city, has been working on a Mother's Day Out Program with young mothers in the community of the suburban building.

(5) It may or may not have enabled us to save money. The real question is, can we have a better congregational life because we have a greater variety of people and the opportunity for a more diversified and richer sense of congregational mission?"

If this question can be answered in the affirmative and if there is sufficient strength, the multi-location church would be a reasonable option for consideration.

Multiple Sessions

When a congregation begins to outgrow its facilities, the only solution offered in practically all cases is that of adding more space. When a church must rebuild or relocate, the typical desire is for room sufficient to accommodate all those who could be present on a sunny Easter Sunday. In both of these cases, an assumption is made that space needs to be provided to handle everyone *at the same time.* Some Protestant congregations are now questioning this assumption.

For years the procedure of multiple sessions has been common among Roman Catholics. Most parishes have three, four, or more services each Sunday. In commercial pursuits, multiple use of large spaces is an economic necessity. Theaters often have two showings in the afternoon and three or four in the evening. In a modern sports arena, there may be ice-skating lessons and hockey in the morning, a basketball game in the afternoon, and a boxing match in the evening. Very few organizations can afford to build large, expensive buildings for use one or two hours a week. The church will probably not be able to afford this much longer.

A starting point in thinking about this option is to realize that little fellowship really takes place during a typical worship service. The main purpose is to worship God. Even during the "friendliness moment" nothing substantial can happen in the way of fellowship because of the number of people present and the fact that they are usually sitting in straight rows looking at the back of many heads. Fellowship occurs before and after the service in small, conversational groupings. Therefore, besides the purely egotistical/numbers fascination of seeing everyone at the same time, there seem to be very few logical reasons why multiple sessions will not work as satisfactorily as one session.

When a church considers changing to two services, the objection is often heard that such a procedure will "split the congregation in two." This does not need to happen, however, if there is a deliberate effort to provide all-church fellowship apart from the worship services. This can be accomplished in a variety of ways, including dinners, picnics, trips, and parties. If there is a need for such intermingling to occur on Sunday mornings, a stand-up fellowship time (tea and talk, coffee and conversation, lemonade lull) can be scheduled between services in the fellowship area of the building. Churches with multiple services often find that more real fellowship actually takes place under these conditions than when there was but one service.

One reason for moving to multiple sessions is the variety that can be offered. Even if the services are identical, the different times give people a choice. Practically every church that changes to more than one service experiences an increase in attendance. Variety in the type of worship or education gives an added incentive. Few congregations are homogeneous. There is a wide range of customs, likes, and dislikes in the diverse church of today. In other areas of life-style, such as wearing apparel, food, travel, housing, recreation, entertainment, education, and vocation, people may select among many options that which best meets their needs. Multiple services give the creative congregation opportunity to affirm and celebrate its unique characteristics which are a gift from God.

Another reason for multiple sessions is, of course, economic. Any church can nearly double its attendance capacity at no increase in capital cost by moving to two sessions. As has been mentioned previously, provision must be made at the same time for the important fellowship aspect. Likewise, the church school capacity can also be greatly increased if sessions are held simultaneously with the worship services. For this, care must be taken in scheduling so that there are as few minor inconveniences as possible for families with children in several age groups.

If a new building is being planned for multiple sessions, it is difficult to cut costs in half, because members do not attend the services in equal numbers. However, a strong educational effort regarding the stewardship benefits can help change attendance habits. A 65–35 percent attendance split can still result in substantially lower costs. Experience has shown that construction savings in the neighborhood of 30 to 35 percent are possible when there are multiple services. This benefit makes the option worth serious consideration. In addition, there are savings on utility bills and the consumption of irreplaceable natural resources.

A popular way of approaching multiple sessions is to schedule them in a series, that is, for example, an early worship service followed by church school and a later service. This has advantages in existing buildings that were not originally designed for more than one usage. Worship and church school at the same time without adequate acoustical control can be far from satisfactory. Sound can carry through floors, walls, and ducts if they were improperly designed. If remodeling can correct these deficiencies, however, or in the case of new construction, creative design can enhance the many advantages of simultaneous sessions.

Simultaneous sessions allow the members to arrive at the same time. Ideally, half go to church school while the other half worship. When the first session of worship and education concludes, the people exchange places. Those in worship go to church school classes and vice versa. A twenty- to thirty-minute period of fellowship (with refreshments, if desired) in between sessions allows the whole church family to see and interact with one another.

A common objection to multiple sessions is the belief that more ushers, teachers, and choir members will be needed. In most cases, however, the leadership required is proportional to the number of people served, not the number of services held. Churches moving to multiple sessions often increase attendance and, because of that, require more leaders. This is an advantage in that opportunities are provided for new members and those who are less active to participate more fully in the life of the church.

Although two worship services may be quite different from each other because of the variety of needs to be met, there should be no indication that one is the "major attraction" or "main event" while the other is less important. To equalize the services, some congregations have their senior choir rotate between the two, or sing periodically at both. The same procedure can be followed with special celebrative events, such as baptism, dedication, or confirmation. If the church is large enough, classes for all ages would be available during each session. If certain age groups cannot be accommodated at both hours, selection should be made carefully according to the predominant age of member families. An adult class should be available during each session.

Good building design will allow, even encourage, a successful experience in moving to multiple sessions. If these sessions are held simultaneously, sound transmission and circulation are important factors for consideration. The Space Relationship Diagram shows how the large central narthex provides room for circulation and fellowship as well as being an adequate sound buffer for simultaneous sessions. (See the next chapter for more information on the narthex.) Experience has shown that there seems to be a psychological barrier to growth when worship or class attendance reaches about 80 percent of capacity on a regular basis. When this point is reached, serious consideration of the multiple-session concept could result in the shifting of more resources from construction of buildings to programs meeting the needs of people.

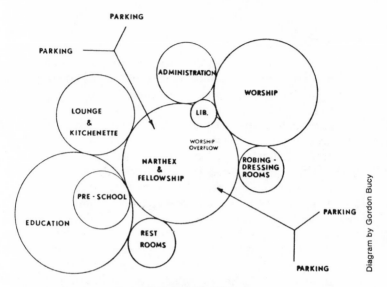

Space Relationship Diagram

The Multi-Phase Building

Each of the three previously discussed planning options can apply to either new or existing structures. A church wishing to function in more than one place can share space in both locations or build anew. Churches desiring to share a building can utilize new or recycled facilities, or even a combination of the two, as is illustrated in Mankato, Minnesota (see page 36). A congregation can move to multiple/simultaneous sessions in either existing or new space. Now, as we turn to multi-phase buildings, it needs to be recognized that thoughtful master planning must take place before construction begins if the result is to be satisfactory.

Additions that were not adequately planned usually have aesthetic and functional problems. In appearance, they are often unattractive and exhibit unbalanced proportions. Inside, a common weakness is an extremely poor circulation pattern. As an example, there are hundreds of pseudo-colonial church buildings across the country with educational space added at the rear. Thus, worshipers either enter the sanctuary from up front beside the chancel area or else go through the basement to enter at the back.

When the funds are not available to meet all building needs at one time, competent professional architectural talent can design a total plan that is attractive and also functions well during each phase. Each stage must be able to stand on its own while still being so designed that it plays a supporting role within the final building complex. This accomplishment is a true work of art requiring a high level of creative energy.

In the beginning, the key congregational decision is that of program priorities. Which program is of greatest importance to the future of the church, or are all equally significant? Since it is quite likely that all spaces in the first phase will need to be flexible, which section of the building is most conducive to use for a variety of programs? Which part of the master plan provides the most usable program space for the money?

Answers to questions such as these will determine both feasibility and the sequential order of phasing. With adequate acoustical treatment, the same space in the first phase can be utilized for both worship and education. The ceiling in this area should be kept as low as practical because of the difficulty and extra cost of sound and visual control when there is excess height. Double usage requires that all seating and other furniture be movable. This rearranging of furniture can take place in ten to fifteen minutes between the church school and worship hours. The time and effort required for rearranging is more than justified by construction cost savings and increased program flexibility.

The acoustical requirements of worship and educational space are quite different. Singing and the use of musical instruments, such as organ or piano, require some sound reverberation while teaching sessions require sound absorption. Thus, the ability to tune the first phase area acoustically is very important. This can be accomplished through the use of attractive, reversible panels on the wall or as a part of movable space dividers. One side of the panel is a hard surface to reflect sound while the other side is carpet, drapery material, acoustical tile, or some other sound-absorbing material. The size and placement of such panels can be determined by a competent acoustical engineer. If needed, adjustments may be made after several months of use.

There is also a system available to sound-tune a space electronically. This is accomplished through a narrow band equalization process which allows selective elimination of reverberation, feedback, ring, etc., according to the way the space is being used at the time. The electronic system has the potential of saving costs for structural, architectural, or furnishing modifications.

Other means of controlling sound and vision include multiple-storage units and chalkboards (which can have sound-absorbing material on the back), lower ceilings around the perimeter of the room, carpeted floors, acoustical ceiling tile, or masking background noise such as that from a fountain. Whatever means are used, it is possible to design a first phase in which one large space is used for both worship and education. Additional minimal requirements include one or two separate nursery rooms for small children, an office-study which may also function as a classroom, mechanical space, and rest rooms. A kitchenette may also be desired to serve snacks or meals in the large, flexible space.

When a building is phased, there is usually a portion of a wall or the end of a corridor which is designed to be removed as easily as possible so that the next section may be added. Since there will be some additional cost for this removal, the connecting section should be as small as good design will allow. Because the color and texture of construction material change through the years, especially brick and stone, it is wise to design the connecting surfaces of materials that might more easily match. Since it is relatively simple to match paints, wood is a good possibility, or else a window area. A balance in each section of two or three exterior materials, such as wood, brick, and glass, also simplifies the matching process. With careful design, the phasing of a building need not be overly obvious when it is completed.

Because of its versatility, the large narthex (discussed in the next chapter) makes a good central core for the first phase. Typically, the sanctuary is the most expensive area of the church building. Therefore, since space per dollar is usually crucial, the sanctuary is seldom chosen as the section to build first. The traditional fellowship hall has proven to be a rather impractical space since it is not often utilized for large attendance programs and, with its normally high ceiling and hard surfaces, it is not acoustically or aesthetically conducive to use for Christian education classes. When designed properly, the central narthex provides a pleasant, warm area for worship without the cost of high roof spans and permanent furnishings as found in most sanctuaries.

With adequate sound control, the narthex can accommodate several youth and adult church school classes. Furthermore, with a kitchen adjacent, fellowship meals and other informal events can be handled. If the central narthex is chosen for the first phase, it is often accompanied by some classrooms and administrative space. The second phase may then become the remainder of the educational and administrative facility, with the sanctuary as the final phase.

The timing of each phase should relate to actual needs. Congregational growth often occurs at a rate different from that originally expected. Some churches have been severely handicapped by overbuilding. For the sake of good stewardship, options such as multiple sessions should be considered or utilized before adding another section to the building.

The master plan is a guide which allows functional and aesthetically pleasing expansion of a church facility. It is not sacred and inflexible. When the time comes for expansion, compare the design of the next phase with the requirements at that time. Some adjustment of the original master plan is usually possible.

Multiple phases allow a congregation to move forward when the time is ripe for new programs or a fruitful ministry in a different location even when funds for the total building are not available. The experiences of a number of churches indicate that it is not wise to delay action until sufficient resources accumulate to complete the entire project at one time. Neither has it proven helpful to construct the "shell" of the building in the hopes of completing it over the years. Such space is not appealing, and the mortgage payments often delay completion beyond the time of opportunity. Both of these options can lead to church stagnation or even death. A flexible, well-designed first phase can function as if it were much more space, meeting the needs and allowing the church to move forward.

The Buildingless Church

Each of the previous options requires some type of ecclesiastical building. The building may be new, used, or remodeled, but it is a structure separate from homes, schools, and community centers. Now an option that requires no separate building will be briefly considered. The purpose is only to point out that such an option is available, not to examine the subject exhaustively.[4] However, while

---

[4]A more complete review of house churches may be found in Charles M. Olsen, *The Base Church* (Atlanta: Forum House, Publishers, 1973); Donald R. Allen, *Barefoot in the Church* (Atlanta: John Knox Press, 1972); "House Church One" and "House Church Two" in the *Chicago Seminary Register;* Philip and Phoebe Anderson, *The House Church* (Nashville: Abingdon Press, 1975).

this idea often receives much theoretical support, there are very few contemporary success stories of such groups that endure for more than a few years.

Although Christians have constructed worship buildings for centuries, it is obvious that such places are not essential to the exercise of the faith. Several references are made in the New Testament to the "church in your house." Until the time of Constantine in the early fourth century, Christians either borrowed space or met in homes or caves for their services. Severe persecution as well as a lack of funds prevented permanent construction, since most of the early believers were very poor. Only when the faith was legitimatized by governmental authorities did there arise enough of a sense of security to build separate ecclesiastical structures.

Amazingly, it did not take long for church buildings to assume a much greater than warranted position of prominence for Christians. The unjustified separation of "sacred" from "secular" space appeared, along with excessive emphasis on materialism. The towering, magnificent, ornate, expensive cathedral arose as an other-worldly island surrounded by oceans of poverty and suffering. Early in the Protestant Reformation simpler church buildings were a marked contrast to the splendid cathedrals, but soon the same excesses arose even among the majority of the reformers. A small group, particularly among the Anabaptists, met in homes in an attempt to re-create the New Testament church.

As a reaction against the cost and pride associated with the typical, seldom-used church facility, a small minority of Christians today are functioning without such separate space. The reasons for this style also include frustration with the priorities of the traditional church and the desire for lay persons to participate more actively in the ministry.

One group in Rochester, New York, states its purpose in this way:

> . . . a group of people with religious roots were feeling a need for a more intimate community where we could care, be cared for and *grow*. Efforts to find this within the traditional church had taken on the character of trying to fit a round peg into a square hole, creating only rough edges, sawdust and heartache. Uneasily, but with enthusiasm we decided to try a house church.
>
> There were, and are, sacrifices in this commitment. We chose to leave comforting tradition, the quiet and majesty of a formal sanctuary, organ music, and more.

We are all ministers, record keepers, Christian education directors, musicians, etc., so we can't depend on *the* minister to make things happen or have the service ready at the appointed hour of worship. We are the church.[5]

Regarding the materialistic aspect, this same congregation says:

We also felt a need to put aside the overwhelming burden of property. Buildings and their trappings can often loom so large that the Kingdom of God gets lost somewhere between the AV equipment and the silver tea service. We try with fair success to collect no belongings. We travel lightly.

Before church was a building and now church is people.[6]

Because they "travel light," the buildingless church can give more. Often, over 50 percent of the budget goes to outreach and missions. There is also a great deal of flexibility and the opportunity to involve all ages in the action. There are, of course, imperfections in this as in any other option.

The buildingless church may be defined as a unit of congregational life which is small enough to facilitate the development of meaningful interpersonal relationships, basic enough to engage in mission action, and large enough to be visible in the world as the Body of Christ. It is an assembling of small groups of persons in homes or public buildings gathered for the purpose of being the living church. Some are individual, house churches. Others include several small groups which assemble together periodically for celebration. Because the tenor of our time calls for collaboration and cooperation, the house church cluster offers a viable model. This concept seems to be most valid in urban or suburban settings.

The Reformed Church in America has made plans for such a buildingless community, called Eutychus. It is aimed at "that great, unrecognized throng who are sleeping in our church windows, doorways and pews; who fall from our sanctuaries and trip over our terminology. They challenge our ability to awaken them before they fall and revive them after they have hit the ground."

A house church cluster is sometimes started intentionally when a new congregation is born, as was the case with the Agora Community in St. Paul, Minnesota. At other times it is response to growth. When the Philadelphia Gospel Temple outgrew its facility, house churches

[5]*The House Church,* Introductory Pamphlet (Rochester, N.Y.), p 3.
[6]*Ibid.,* pp. 5, 14.

were started rather than making a move to bigger buildings. Around forty groups meet on a weekly basis, with the entire cluster assembling together approximately every three months. Homes, schools, and other existing church buildings are used for various meetings.

Any congregation which contemplates facility changes should consider the buildingless church option. As the few preceding examples suggest, it can work and does allow the placing of more resources into people-centered programs.

Sharing Space with Commercial Operations

Because of their unique circumstances, a few urban churches have successfully utilized areas within business buildings. One congregation in the Northeast occupies a high-rise building in which several floors are used for offices. A church in the South is located on the top floors of an apartment building. These congregations felt that they had valid reasons to continue ministering to their densely populated communities. An office or apartment building houses people who are a potential constituency. The cost of leasing space could well be less than that of purchasing land, constructing, and maintaining a separate building. Renting also allows a degree of flexibility to meet changing needs and neighborhoods.

High costs for land, buildings, and maintenance are no longer unique. Such circumstances are becoming all too common and demand great creativity in seeking solutions. The leasing (or purchasing) of space within an office, condominium, or apartment complex is one possibility. Sometimes a "trade-off" can occur which is beneficial to both parties. For example, a condominium or apartment recreation room may be used for worship and church meetings with the understanding that the pastor will serve as the chaplain-on-call responding to the needs of residents. Obviously, the congregation considering such a possibility will be one which finds its identity in its fellowship and ministries to people rather than in ecclesiastical buildings and property.

Another possibility is that of sharing property with some compatible type of commercial operation. The experience of the Arlington Temple (Methodist), Arlington, Virginia, illustrates a broad definition of compatibility! This congregation had property in a desirable location for their ministry but lacked sufficient funds to erect a needed building. At the same time, a service station across the street was losing its lease. So, thought the pastor, why not blend temporal and spiritual needs of the neighborhood by combining a gas station with a church building? If the oil company would agree to a long-term lease as well as pay a royalty on each gallon of gasoline sold, it could have a new station in the same area. The company accepted and occupied part of the ground-level space under the church building! Only slight modifications were needed in the building to meet code requirements. The gas station closes on Sundays but is in operation when many activities are going on in the rooms above it. This arrangement worked well and enabled the church to build, providing a monthly income to apply to the mortgage.

When giving consideration to leasing space to businesses, the church should engage an attorney to investigate the legal ramifications. There should be no threat to the nonprofit, tax exempt status of the church if income from leased space is reported as "unrelated business income." Taxes should be paid on that income and on that part of the building which is leased out. If the leased space is also used by the church on Sundays or at other agreed-upon times, the local authorities may work out an agreement based upon an equitable percentage ratio. Churches have leased space to other nonprofit organizations without experiencing difficulty. While open to varying interpretations and in need of thorough research, this option is still worth taking seriously because the current inflationary drain of resources requires congregations to find a variety of new ways to live and minister in the future.

Perhaps an example of property sharing which could be found often in the future is that of St. Peter's Lutheran Church in New York City. Like many downtown churches, membership and giving had greatly declined. The building was deteriorating and costly to maintain. In the late 1960s, a new pastor started programs that ministered in a relevant way to the needs of the neighborhood and, for the first time in years, membership began to increase. The option of relocation had been considered, but now the church decided there was a valid ministry in its present neighborhood. The pastor summed up this revitalized feeling by paraphrasing the Jewish theologian, Abraham Heschel: "Our role is not to retreat back to the catacombs, but to become more human in skyscrapers."

So the church turned down a very healthy offer for the outright sale of its property and waited until a sharing agreement could be made with the large bank which eventually purchased the entire block. Because of the value of its land, the church now shares ownership, condominium-style, of enough property for its fine new building as a part of the total development of the area. The building was paid for by the value of the land with enough left over to support vital programs for years to come. All of this was possible only through the condominium sharing arrangement.

A 1973 study in the downtown area of Boston found that "the institutional Church, regardless of denomination, faces a situation in the urban community that can be described only as disastrous.... All of the churches in the inner city with which we have had discussions are in some measure of trouble."[7] Many urban areas are over-churched, and so a high percentage of these congregations will be forced to merge or disband. If every church relocates, the suburbs will become overchurched as well. However, even those remaining urban churches that have sufficient membership for valid ministries will find survival difficult. One possibility for relieving some financial pressure is to engage in a sharing arrangement with a public or commercial organization. (Since leases can be broken, a church should not rely upon such income for long-range debt retirement.)

Ministries are possible in busy commercial areas or shopping centers. People become ill, undergo stress, have breakdowns, and face crises there every day. Workers and shoppers need child care in such areas. On coffee breaks or at lunch, there is opportunity for discussion groups, learning experiences, counseling. Seldom is the church present to help meet such needs, however, because there is not enough financial support to maintain the traditional, building-centered program. A mutually beneficial sharing arrangement with some commercial operation could reduce overhead expenses to the point that needed Christian ministries may be continued.

[7] *Report on Alternate Uses of Certain Church-Owned Properties in the City of Boston* by The Cheswick Center and the Boston Municipal Research Bureau, 1973, p. 18. Used with permission.

Flexible Space 3

Church buildings that are too large or utilized only sparingly are a great detriment to effective ministry. Typically, such facilities contain single-use spaces that were relatively expensive to build and are costly to use and maintain. Thus, in effect, these structures siphon funds and energy away from people-centered programs. Designing for multiple use can keep the church from overbuilding and therefore allow a larger portion of the budget to be used for Christian ministries.

Financial problems are increasing rapidly for many churches. The budget crunch is being felt everywhere. One aspect of the crunch is that, because of inflation, higher salaries are necessary to find and retain talented ministers. "Every year hundreds of full-time ministerial positions either disappear completely or become part-time positions because that congregation no longer can afford to keep up with the rapid increase in salaries . . . today, relatively few congregations with an average attendance of less than 125 at worship are able to justify a full-time salary."[1]

Today's stewardship requires that flexible space become a high priority in the construction of church buildings. The planning options covered in the preceding chapter are most effective when the spaces utilized are flexible. However, an uneasy feeling seems to surface whenever church members think about multi-use facilities. While the financial motivation is strongly appealing and organiza-

---

[1] Lyle E. Schaller, *The Parish Paper*, September, 1977. Used with permission.

tions other than the church are observed using flexible space successfully at a major savings in capital, it appears to be a struggle to transfer these positive feelings over to the church. Perhaps the reason for this is a continuing concern about some kind of distinction between secular and sacred space.

For some Christians, the separation between sacred and secular things ended when the temple curtain was torn in two (Matthew 27:51). From that moment on, access to the holy was unlimited. Instead of just certain things or places being sacred, every thing and place had the potential of being sacred. For other believers, however, the separation between sacred and secular apparently still exists. Portions of the church building, or sometimes all of it, are reserved exclusively for particular "religious" functions. When questioned as to why, the answers clearly imply the belief that some places and things are more sacred than others. Perhaps such feelings arise from memories associated with these places.

Speaking to this issue, Robert E. Rambusch has stated: "Many people see the religious multi-purpose building as an uneasy compromise between the sacred and the profane, the temple and the money-changers, the extraordinary and ordinary. They fail to see that a multi-purpose building can incarnate the transcendent in the every day." To state this in another way, fellowship and dining can occur in a church sanctuary if there is an openness to receiving God through the conversation and the food as well as through the worship service. The attitude is of considerably more significance than the locale.

When they take the time to think about it, Christians want to avoid all forms of idolatry, including that which makes a church building an object of worship. Christians want to see God as One who is unlimited in time and space, able to permeate all of life rather than being confined to a brief weekly appearance at the corner of First and Main Streets. "It is our responsibility, not to select certain places and call them holy, but to see the whole world as holy and therefore manage it, care for it, and put it in the kind of order that reflects a conviction that the whole earth is the House of God."[2] By accepting the attitude that the holy may be present everywhere, multipurpose space becomes a practical solution to present economic pressures and an opportunity to embody a more inclusive concept of what is sacred.

[2] Edward A. Sovik, from an address given at the International Congress on Art and Architecture, Brussels, Belgium, September, 1970. Quoted with permission.

Requirements for Adequate Flexible Space

It might be argued that a barn or aircraft hanger is the ultimate in flexibility. Actually, large open areas are often very restrictive in their usages. The closest the church today comes to this type of space is in the fellowship hall or gymnasium. Typically, these rooms have hard surfaces all around and high ceilings, resulting in a relatively long sound reverberation time. Thus, conversation is difficult due to a hollow, echoing effect. The high ceilings make the use of movable dividers very difficult. It is nearly impossible to provide adequate circulation paths through and around such a room when it is occupied. When two or more groups are using such large, open spaces, there are normally distractions of sight and sound.

An area may rightfully be called adequate multi-use space when it can *effectively* provide room for two or three different programs. While it is easier to meet the standards in a new building, existing structures can often be economically adapted. One basic requirement is that the floor should be level. A sloped, auditorium-style floor allows only fixed seats aimed toward a stage or platform. What can happen in such space is severely limited, usually to the observation of a performance or presentation. The physical restraints typically result in a one-way movement of ideas and information.

Another requirement for multipurpose space is the judicious location of load-bearing walls and columns. For new construction, this criteria should be a part of the early, pre-architectural planning. For existing buildings, the plans and specifications will show what constraints there are in this regard. True flexibility can be prevented by a lack of forethought in designing the structural elements of a building.

Related to the structure is the requirement that there be adjacent, accessible spaces on the same building level. A facility that is highly flexible allows spaces to "flow" into each other as particular needs arise. Rooms that are adjacent may have very different purposes so far as their main usage is concerned. However, if the floors are level and the dividing wall (or part of it) can be made movable, the total space may be utilized for a variety of purposes. Such flexible use requires that the furnishings be easily movable. In a church building, such items as the sanctuary seating, the chancel and its furnishings, choir risers, tables, chairs, and storage units need to be movable.

Multipurpose space requires well-designed acoustical control

ACOUSTICAL CONTROL

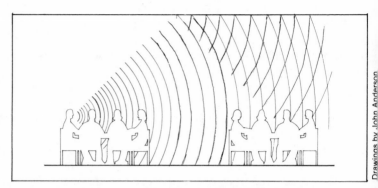

Drawings by John Anderson

Adjacent spaces without acoustical treatment

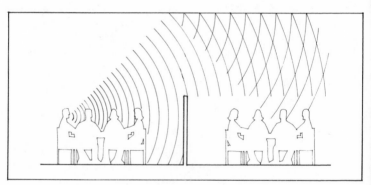

Use of a sound screen only, such as a movable door

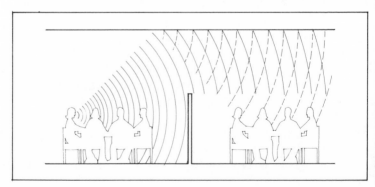

Use of acoustical ceiling and sound screen

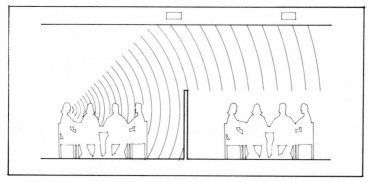

Use of acoustical ceiling, sound screen, and masking sound from another source, such as music or a fountain

through such means as careful selection of the finish materials, ceiling height, carpet, and high-quality folding doors. Excess noise cannot be allowed to disturb other programs going on nearby at the same time (see illustration). Good visual control is also needed. This can be accomplished by using movable panels, furnishings, folding doors and judiciously locating the hallways. People must be able to move easily from one area to another without passing through or so close to another area that a distraction is caused.

Flexibility is enhanced when it is possible to isolate certain sections of the building. Some programs that the church may decide to sponsor are quite "public" in nature and have the potential of creating conflict if all space needs are not carefully resolved. For example, a multipurpose space which houses a youth program during the week may attract more people if there is a separate access which does not require passing through other sections of the building. This may also be desired for custodial and security reasons. Spaces which can be separated in this way when needed should have their own heating-cooling controls and toilets. Multipurpose space which is used more frequently during the week may also require that special attention be given to the parking situation since churches often use parking spaces on Sunday which are not available other days.

The Financial Advantages of Flexible Space

In recent years, construction costs increased at a rate estimated to be 3 to 7 percent higher than that of the economy as a whole. Because of the large spaces usually needed and their unique program requirements, church buildings are relatively complex and high priced. Architects and contractors consider church buildings more similar to hospitals than to schools, for example, and thus usually charge higher fees for church design. The few repetitive spaces, relatively small size of most projects, and comparatively low volume in the church building field all tend to make prices higher. Before deciding to enter a building program, all churches should thoroughly investigate options other than construction and compare possible facility costs with those for staff, programs, and missions. If it is determined that construction is warranted in spite of inflation and extremely high land and building costs, the church would be wise to plan as much multipurpose space as possible.

It may be helpful to apply a new procedure in determining the cost of a building relating to its flexibility and subsequent frequency of use. Traditionally, cost has been figured on the basis of dollars per square foot. However, that does not take into account the important element of *frequency of use*. One building may cost 50 percent more than another; but because of its design for flexibility and the many church programs that are therefore possible, it is used three times as often. Such a structure is returning much more per dollar than the "cheaper" building in terms of *usage cost* per square foot.

Taking a figure of $50 per square foot as an example of construction prices and one week as a standard measure of time for this purpose, a church building that is occupied only once a week would have a usage cost of $50 per square foot. But, used twice a week, such as with simultaneous sessions of worship and church school, the usage cost would be $50 divided by two, or $25 per square foot. Many fellowship halls are, in practice, fully occupied only about once a month; so their usage cost would be very high: $50÷¼=$200 per square foot! In contrast, a fully flexible space that can be utilized five days a week for programs, such as worship, fellowship, meetings, and day care, would have a usage cost of $50 ÷ 5 = $10 per square foot. This concept gives a more accurate measure of the actual value received per dollar than does a straight square footage figure.

If the church is to be effective in the future, it must strongly challenge traditional habits that are based more on culture than on

Scripture. Americans are fascinated by the size and expanse of things, from endless deserts to massive crowds of people, from sprawling mountain ranges to large buildings. Western culture has equated bigness with success while the Bible tells of God's concern for the smallest sparrow. Are church members ready to move, not toward retrenchment, but toward providing adequate space with no wasteful excess?

A church building in the Midwest has a second-floor sanctuary at the top of a long flight of stairs, one large meeting room which also must serve as a traffic thoroughfare to all sections of the facility, and a dark, damp, wide-open basement. Designed carefully for multipurpose use, a replacement structure of half the size could actually be of much more service than is the current building. There would be half as much initial investment and the interest saved over a 10- to 15-year loan period would be in the tens of thousands of dollars.

In addition to savings on construction and loan interest, the congregation which resists the temptation to overbuild will save much on utilities and maintenance. It is possible for a well-designed, multipurpose building to perform as effectively as a structure nearly twice its size. Thus the portion that is not constructed will never need such things as a new roof, replacement plumbing fixtures, or gas or oil for heating. With an estimated annual inflation factor of 10 percent, each $100 that it is not necessary to spend on utilities or maintenance bills this year will save $1,573 in ten years.

Sometimes, the Planning Committee can be highly influenced by the appeal to save money with the use of a "stock plan" or "pre-fab church building." A warning needs to be given that organizations offering such plans are usually much more sophisticated in their sales techniques than they are in their provision of useful, truly economical space. While initial construction costs may be lower, there are no such plans available, to date, that provide the real and continuing economy of multipurpose use. Spaces are single use and very traditional in design. While it is hoped that improvements will come, at present a building designed specifically for the program needs of a particular church and with built-in flexibility will be the most useful and economical over the years.

Financially, it makes a great deal of sense to have all church buildings multipurpose. As has been observed, there is nothing in New Testament teachings to prevent this. The issue is whether Christians can overcome their "pride of place" and the false sacred-secular distinction concerning the use of church buildings. If they can, there would be more resources available for ministries to hurting people. Basically, this is a matter of priorities.

Specific Applications of Flexible Space

Churches have used the concept of flexible space for some time. Some applications have proven to be much more usable than others. In planning for flexible space, a church needs to evaluate rather carefully the advantages and disadvantages of these particular approaches

The Sanctuary

The sanctuary seems to be the one area that church members often object to using for anything other than worship. Yet it is typically the largest, most expensive room in the building. If a congregation has but one worship service a week, the usage cost per square foot is quite high. Perhaps a prayer meeting, Bible study, or choir practice is also held there regularly, but seldom is a space that big actually needed for such events. A big wedding or funeral requires such a large room periodically, depending upon the size and age of the congregation.

That very word "sanctuary" implies something sacred to most Christians. However, we need to reflect upon what it is that is truly sacred. Is it not the encounter between people and God that is sacred rather than the place where worship and prayer happen to occur? When two people are united together, is it not the marriage vows which are sacred, rather than the floor, walls, and roof within which the vows are exchanged? Weddings held in gardens or outdoor chapels can be just as valid and Christian as those that take place in ornate cathedrals. The same is true with worship, which can occur in a variety of settings.

The same wood, nails, bricks, and other materials of construction may be used to build a public school or a sanctuary, a tavern or a place of worship. It is the people present and their purpose for being there which makes an event special, not the setting in which it is held. Granted, the setting is often manipulated in an attempt to make people respond in a desired way, but this is a questionable tactic for Christians. God confronted Paul while he was walking down the road and Peter while he was fishing. God speaks in a variety of ways and at unexpected times. Christians probably highly overrate the influence of so-called "sacred" spaces. Often forgotten are the simplicity and power in that statement "where two or three are gathered in my name, there am I in the midst of them" (Matthew 18:20).

Acceptance of this concept does not mean that churches are relieved of the obligation to provide spaces for worship. However, there are two implications which relate directly to this discussion. First, it is not required that the place be used *exclusively* for worship. Second, the space can change to meet the need. In other words, a large area is usually needed for public worship on Sundays, a smaller space for weekday services, and perhaps a room the size of an individual office for quiet prayer and meditation at other times. Different spaces can be used as the requirements change, or sections of the same space can be sized according to the need by using movable dividers.

As was stated earlier in this chapter, requirements for multipurpose worship space include a level floor, movable seating, satisfactory circulation patterns, and the ability to match acoustics to the particular use. In an existing building, a sloping floor offers the greatest resistance to change. At best, leveling the floor is both difficult and expensive. In some cases, due to the design, it is impossible. When the floor is already level, however, real change can occur. An old Episcopal church in downtown St. Louis replaced the fixed pews in its building with movable chairs several years ago. This has allowed a variety of worship programs to be held that were impossible in the past, as well as such events as community concerts.

There are those who still maintain that a sloping floor is necessary for good visibility. It is not the slope of the floor, however, but the proper angle between the eye of the worshiper and the worship leader, choir or baptismal candidate, that is essential for visibility. There are at least three ways to achieve a satisfactory angle of vision. One way is to slope the floor, which is costly and renders flexible use of the worship space impossible. A second way is to elevate the worship leaders' area to a height which mades them visible from the back row. This is much less expensive and does not leave a space inflexible. (See illustration.) If the chancel is built in sections so that it is movable, its height can be properly designed for the size of the room and may even be raised or lowered to account for the number of people present if it is designed for that purpose.

A third option for achieving good visibility from seats on the level floor of a new building is to design the shape of the worship area

VISIBILITY OF SPEAKER

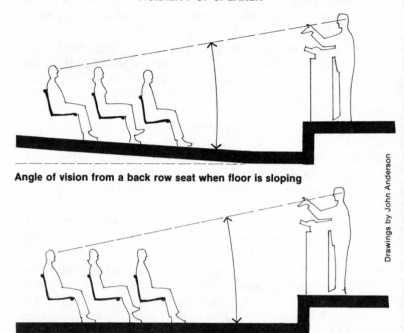

Angle of vision from a back row seat when floor is sloping

Drawings by John Anderson

With a flat floor, the angle of vision is exactly the same.
Relatively minor adjustments in the height of the platform will result in good vision from the back row in most worship spaces.

in a square or round configuration rather than as a long, narrow, rectangular nave. Then, instead of the last seat being twenty-five rows away from the worship leader, for example, the same number of people can be accommodated in ten or twelve rows. In that kind of design, the worship leaders' area would require only about half as much elevation for good visibility. In addition, the worshipers would be much closer with the opportunity of feeling like participants in the event rather than spectators.

There are now many types of attractive, comfortable, movable seats or pews available for the sanctuary. It should be noted that pews attached to the floor are a relatively recent, mainly American tradition. Most church buildings in Europe for centuries have used chairs as seating (or the worshipers stand throughout the service). Although they have a stake in continuing the American tradition, most pew manufacturers see the growing trend and now offer at least one type of flexible seating. These movable seats can be cushioned, have spaces for hymnbooks and Communion cups, and some type of easily removable ganging device. Some of the chairs are stackable for storage purposes.

Even if a church limits its flexible use of space to a variety of worship programs, movable seating is necessary. The seating direction can be changed according to the program need. Chairs can face the pulpit, the choir, the baptistry or font. Communion, or the entire service, can be held "in the round." Part of the service can be devoted to small group discussion or Bible study. If a religious drama is being presented, the arrangement of stage and audience can be according to the requirements of the specific play. For a wedding, the couple can have a central aisle, or two aisles leading to the chancel area, or whatever is desired. For funerals, there is no worry about having enough room for the casket wherever the family wishes it to be located.

Flexible seating also allows a degree of latitude in determining the seating capacity of the worship area. It is possible to move the rows of chairs closer together or add seats at the ends of rows to increase the total capacity. (Care must be taken not to restrict access to exits or in other ways violate fire and safety codes.) At other times, when smaller than normal attendance is expected, the seats can be spread out to give that "full" appearance which seems to have some psychological advantages. (The carpet or other flooring material can also receive more even wear across its total surface when movable seating is periodically rearranged.)

The key to full flexibility in the sanctuary is acceptance of the proposition that the space and traditional furnishings themselves are not inherently sacred and thus may be utilized for purposes other than worship. Because worship is the main use for sanctuary space and has certain acoustical, visual, and other program requirements, the list of additional purposes may need to be limited to those which are compatible. However, there are enough such uses that the church which accepts this concept usually finds it possible to make a major shifting of resources from building-centered concerns to people-centered programs.

To illustrate the subjects of space compatibility and incompatibility, it is known that programs of active recreation require hard walls for balls to hit, a concrete or tile floor for traction in running, allowing balls to bounce, etc., and coverings over lights and glass for protection. Thus, although it might be possible to make the transitional changes necessary, an active recreation program is generally incompatible with the space required for programs of worship. On the other hand, programs such as education, fellowship, and small group meetings can use spaces properly designed for several functions.

Using the worship area for Christian education classes has been discussed under the multiphase building planning option in chapter 2. Having one or two adult classes meet in the sanctuary is an old idea; but if the space is not designed for flexible use, people usually sit in straight, stiff rows and hear other classes about as well as their own. With careful planning, however, three or four older youth and adult classes can utilize a 250-seat worship space with only minor inconveniences and at a major dollar saving. Chairs can be arranged in a circle; and movable, sound-absorbing partitions can provide acoustical and visual isolation. Care needs to be taken in placement so that people may circulate unobtrusively. Rearrangement of seats can be done in a few minutes before the worship service.

Use of the worship area (or part of it) for fellowship events, such as dinners or receptions, probably offers the greatest potential in terms of dollar savings. There should be no major resistance to doing this if members accept what has already been said about conserving resources, setting priorities, and "sacred, holy" places. It is recognized that widespread acceptance of these concepts does not usually come easily. However, one way that nonbiblical traditions can be changed is through a strong challenge. The future of the church may well depend upon such challenges regarding the use of resources like church buildings.

Adjacent to the worship area is normally a narthex or foyer. If it is of sufficient size and if the opening between is large enough, the worship and narthex areas can flow together to become an attractive fellowship dinner or reception space. A nearby kitchen is, of course, helpful. Folding chairs can be used rather than the movable sanctuary seating, if desired, and tables with folding legs work well and store easily. While the wall surfaces and carpeted floor offer good sound control for fellowship events, concern is often expressed about spilling on the carpet or lingering food odors. Certainly these are both justified concerns.

Food odors can be removed by thorough cleaning, using the air circulation system of the building, and spraying air fresheners.

Commercial grades of carpet are available which are both stain-resistant and attractive. Most spills can be completely removed. If people do not trust the carpet to resist stains, however, there are still two other options. One is to have the carpet installed in sections on rollers located along one or two walls of the room. Then the carpet can be rolled up, when desired, to expose a tile or sealed concrete floor. A Presbyterian church in Missouri has used this arrangement satisfactorily for years. They worship, meet, eat, and even dance in the same room. The other option is basically the reverse of this. Permanent carpeting is installed with rolls of vinyl sheets or other protective materials available that can quickly cover the carpet as needed. Either of these options is considerably less expensive than building twice as much single-use space. The slight inconvenience in periodically rolling and unrolling a covering is minimal when compared to the benefits of conserving resources in this way. However, in most cases, covered or retractable carpet is not really necessary. "First class" restaurants are usually carpeted and many serve three meals a day, 365 days a year.

Large spaces reserved for a small number of uses do not represent good stewardship. Ways must be found to utilize the larger spaces in church buildings more often, and these suggestions speak to that important subject.

Fellowship Halls

When carefully analyzed from a financial point of view, the usage cost per square foot of almost all fellowship halls is unacceptably high, Even when doubling as a gymnasium (which usually does not work unless there is the ability to support at least a half-time youth or recreational director), such space is not a viable option for the vast majority of congregations. More than an ivory tower theory, this is a report from the experiences of many churches. It has been found impractical to attempt to compete with school, YMCA, and city recreational facilities.

From a program point of view, the space provided is often an unsatisfactory compromise. The gym is seldom of standard size, and there are numerous obstructions for balls to encounter. Showers are usually missing. When used for dinners, the hard surfaces result in echoing which makes it difficult to hear the speaker, musical group, or play. The poor acoustics and barn-like atmosphere are not conducive to close, warm fellowship. When two, three, or more classes meet in such space, the high ceiling and hard surfaces make visual and acoustical isolation difficult. Circulation of people is also a problem. (These weaknesses could probably be overcome with sufficient research.)

Before investing hundreds of thousands of dollars in such compromise fellowship space, a church would be wise to determine the programs it can most practically provide for "in-house" as distinguished from those for which it would be best to rent or borrow other existing, public facilities. The number of people expected, the kind of program and its frequency are all important factors. Also significant is the priority of the program as compared with others in attempting to achieve the goals of the congregation.

One day, an out-of-state visitor was being given the "grand tour" of a medium-sized church building. One of the first places visited was the kitchen. An enthusiastic member lovingly extolled the virtues of the gleaming, expensive, stainless steel ovens, triple sink, dish-washer, and other equipment. The visitor inquired as to how often all this magnificent commercial equipment was utilized to prepare a large church meal. The answer was about six times a year, with the trend being downward. The visitor then asked to see the kindergarten classroom and was led to the back of the basement. There, in the dark, former coal bin, right next to the exposed gas furnace, were the little tables and chairs for five-year-olds. Nothing had to be said. The priorities of that church were plainly visible.

This experience was the result of a void in planning. No concerned Christian would purposely choose to give the occasional feeding of the body a higher priority than the regular religious nurturing of developing lives. The goals of a church school class are the same as those of the congregation, and they meet to achieve those goals at least fifty-two times a year, not six. There is really no comparison; yet a lack of planning allowed precious resources to be unwisely distributed. More than other facets of church life, it seems, this area of fellowship-recreation is open to abuse so far as prioritizing and the allocation of resources are concerned. Thus, thorough analysis of both financial implications and program requirements is especially necessary here in the early stages of planning.

Such analysis leads most churches to determine, very early in the process, that provision should be made for only light recreation, such as table games and shuffleboard. A second strong feeling often surfacing is that the only dining space which should be provided is that which is regularly used for other, higher priority programs. In other words, the dining function will be subordinate to other functions for which the space is primarily designed, such as worship, education, and fellowship, and there will be no extra space which is constructed for the single purpose of increasing the meal serving capacity. If more room is needed for a meal, it will be held elsewhere. More stringent public health laws plus decreasing availability of volunteer time from busy working members has resulted in many church dinners being catered or served in restaurants.

Central Narthex

An excellent, multipurpose solution to many space needs is the large, central narthex. This term is defined as "any vestibule leading to the nave." A less ecclesiastical, more appropriate name that has been used for this area is the "gathering place." Although in this book the name "narthex" will continue to be used, it is hoped that a more contemporary, descriptive term will soon come into common usage.

A well-designed, large, central narthex can be one of the most truly multipurpose and significant spaces in a church building. As will be easily observed in the space relationship diagram found on page 44, this area forms the hub around which other spaces develop. When designed in this manner, the narthex replaces several corridors and is the key circulation element in the building. To move from any place to any other, people must travel through the narthex. The design thus helps to provide opportunities for contact, informal fellowship, and conversation.

Ideally, the character of this space should be warmly inviting, similar to the living room of a home. Carpeting can help to give this feeling, as well as provide good sound control. In one corner or at the side, comfortable seating can define a lounge area. Normally, the ceiling is at a height proportionate to the size of the room but not as high as a typical fellowship hall or sanctuary ceiling. While size will vary according to program requirements, the central narthex should be approximately 50 percent as large as the worship area to fulfill its many potential purposes.

One of the major purposes of the narthex is to provide overflow capacity for the sanctuary. Many worship spaces are sized according to the maximum crowd expected. This means that the room is one-third to one-half empty at most services. Because the worship area is so expensive, it is far better stewardship to provide for the average expected attendance and have good overflow space easily available for large crowds. Attractive folding doors or glass partitions between the narthex and sanctuary allow this to happen. Lines of vision and acoustics are planned with the overflow usage in mind.

Another use for the narthex is education. Depending upon its size, from one to four classes (usually adult) are often able to meet in this space. Because of circulation requirements, it is not possible to use the total narthex for classes. Movable dividers and storage units may be utilized to identify the class areas. Some churches have used two walls at the corner of the narthex for library shelves with a folding door allowing the area to be separate or part of the entire room, depending upon the need. Library books have a much greater chance of being read if they are visible and easily accessible. When used for classes or meetings, a thoughtfully designed narthex has enough exits to the outside and to other rooms so that 40 percent or more of its space may be used for classes without hindering circulation.

The large, central narthex becomes an important fellowship area after services. People are able to greet the pastor and each other without feeling cramped or hurried. There is sufficient room to remove, store, and put on coats and various foul-weather gear. If the church has multiple sessions, the narthex provides space for snacks and informal fellowship between services. It is also an ideal location for receptions and receiving lines.

Sanctuary overflow, classes, meetings, library, lounge, fellowship, circulation, receptions—these are some of the major areas which, in many church designs, are given expensive, single-use space. With the large central narthex, all of these uses and more can be adequately provided for in one well-designed, multi-use area.

With folding or roll-away doors to the sanctuary in one direction and to some classrooms in the other, the narthex may also expand to a much greater size as needed. Large fellowship dinners may require that type of expansion on occasion. As was stated earlier, dinners of that magnitude occur infrequently. To provide space for them that does not satisfactorily meet the requirements of one or more regular, weekly programs represents a questionable use of resources. In the large narthex, the requirements of several regular, weekly programs may be met satisfactorily, and the space, plus other flexible areas nearby, is available for large dinners. As the narthex provides overflow space for worship, so the sanctuary can provide overflow space for dinners and other fellowship events. Obviously, a kitchen needs to be located nearby for such meal functions.

While it is naturally easier to design a large, central narthex for a new church building, some existing structures can also be remodeled for this concept. A reasonably large adjacent space, level floors, movable seating, and several openings between load-bearing columns are required to benefit from some of the previously described advantages. Quite a number of existing sanctuaries are too big for their current congregations. In those cases, the back one-third of the room, for example, could be changed into the narthex area. A detailed analysis of costs and advantages and disadvantages should be made before attempting such major changes in an existing building.

Because of its materials of construction, furnishings, the carpeting, ceiling height, and central location, the large narthex is far superior to a traditional fellowship hall. True multipurpose use and economy are provided for fellowship and other program functions.

Christian Education Space

Reference has already been made to using both worship and fellowship space for certain Christian education purposes. Now the opportunities for flexibility within the educational area itself will be examined. It should first be recognized that classes for children through the fourth grade may need to be held in their own separate spaces. In the vast majority of churches, care and education are provided during worship services for children from birth through kindergarten. Many congregations also have such "extended sessions" for older children, sometimes up to those in the sixth grade.

Younger children require a considerable amount of special equipment, and the furnishings are often sized to the age of the child. Therefore, multiple use is usually limited to programs for children of like age. There is a degree of flexibility since children's furnishings and equipment can usually serve an age range of from two to four years. In this category under the general heading of child care come such weekday programs as day care, nursery school, and "mother's day out." To provide successfully for such programs, the experience of many churches indicates that separate storage places are essential. In this way, each group using the space will be accountable for their own supplies and equipment. Another simple suggestion that will help is to provide reversible bulletin boards. Displays can then be left intact because another group can turn the board to the other side for their use.

Day care is a full program for the children of working parents. Many congregations are engaged in such care and thereby provide a needed service to parents while using these classrooms to the maximum extent. A typical day-care program operates from 7 A.M. to 6 P.M. Facilities must meet applicable health, fire, and safety standards. These standards are more strict if public funds are involved. Leadership is given by a salaried, professional staff. Fees are paid by parents and/or social welfare agencies. The church can operate the day-care center on its own or lease space to a group organized for that purpose. In addition to items such as food, salaries, utilities, and maintenance costs necessary to operate a day-care center, an amount for the long-term depreciation (or replacement cost) of the space may be included, if desired. When all of the real costs of operation are included, experience has shown that the regular involvement of around fifty children is required for day care to be fully self-supporting. If the center is not going to pay for itself, the church needs to understand and support the concept that it is providing a subsidized service to the community.

While day care offers the opportunity of fully utilizing children's classrooms, thorough research is necessary to determine if a program beneficial to all can be held. Social service agencies and other day-care centers in the community should be contacted to judge the extent of the need. Starting a program when there is insufficient need can result in the disappointment of unfulfilled expectations and financial loss.

If a sufficiently large program is determined to be feasible, the particular state or municipal code requirements must be matched to the status of the facility. Requirements vary from state to state but usually include items such as: A certain minimum amount of indoor, "ongrade" space per child (often 35 square feet) plus an adequate outdoor play area; a sufficient number of toilets that are easily accessible; a separate room for temporary care of an ill child; an equipped kitchen located relatively close to the classrooms; adequate furnishings and equipment, such as cots for naps, games, toys, playground equipment, first-aid kits, fire extinguishers, fire alarms, and storage closets or cabinets; the number, type, and proper location of building exits to meet safety codes; and a listed telephone. Other requirements include a satisfactory ratio of trained attendants to children, an annual audit of financial records, regular fire drills, physical examinations for all employees, and a daily health inspection of each child.

Although the foregoing list is not complete, it already sounds formidable. However, many existing churches have been licensed to house day-care programs with a relatively minimal expenditure on building improvements. A review of the facility by a representative from the appropriate government licensing agency will indicate what changes, if any, need to be made. If the building presents no major obstacles, the next steps include organization of the governing board, recruitment of leadership, adoption of a budget and fee structure, and advertisement of the dates for enrollment of children.

A nursery school usually offers a program of shorter duration than day care and with some different objectives in mind. If there are two sessions, hours from 9 A.M. to noon and 1 P.M. to 4 P.M. are typical. Children often attend one of the sessions either two or three days per week. Goals include socialization. personal relations, and the beginning development of some basic skills to prepare the child for entrance into school. A nominal fee is charged and leaders are usually paid. Facility requirements are somewhat less than day care because of the shorter time and the fact that snacks, not full meals, are served. The "mother's day out" may be a half-day session every week or two that is more like traditional baby-sitting. Leadership tends to be voluntary and often rotates among the parents involved.

Each of these child-care programs offers the opportunity for greater utilization of younger children's classrooms. When a church builds a new educational facility, consideration should be given to designing it to meet the day-care requirements of the community. Even if that program is never held, these classrooms will allow a better job to be done in Christian education. And, if the decision is made at some later date to sponsor a day-care program, the building will be ready. In considering these possibilities, do not allow the fear of a few smudges on the walls or even an occasional broken window to prevent a program that may be sorely needed. Church buildings are not to be treasured as spotless relics but are meant to be used in the Master's service!

When two or three church school classes form a "department," there are often occasions for having a united meeting of all the classes. Many older educational buildings, based upon the "Akron Plan," held such joint sessions in a large assembly area, then completely vacated that space for small, cell-like classrooms. This procedure represents very poor usage of space, and it is sometimes possible to remodel such buildings for better utilization of the facility. In all program areas of the church building, a few large, multi-use spaces are preferable to many small rooms with immovable walls.

Acoustical folding partitions with sliding seals at the top and bottom make it possible for an assembly to be held within the classroom area itself rather than in a separate, single-use area. When classes are ready to separate, the chairs are rearranged and the partitions closed in just a few minutes. For young people, such partitions may be left open during the week for after-school and evening meetings, light recreation, and fellowship events. Likewise, two or three adjacent adult class areas can open to form a large, comfortable lounge, library, or meeting room. Such space is very useful for retirement-age programs during the week. If next to the narthex, the classroom space may be used for extra dinner seating as required. While good movable doors may cost two or three times as much as a permanent wall, flexibility eliminating several single-use spaces will still result in major construction, utility, and maintenance savings. Less expensive movable doors with a lower acoustical rating may be used, but then more sound-absorbing materials will need to be installed elsewhere to achieve good results.

One hindrance to the flexible use of adult class space is a strong, possessive sense of ownership that often surfaces. A beloved name is placed on the door; comfortable overstuffed chairs are brought in; special curtains are made for the windows; even carpeting is sometimes sealed to the floor. An older adult class may decrease in size yet cling to a large room while a youth or children's class is cramped for space. To overcome this, some churches have standing rules that spaces will be reallocated annually according to need. All classes should have a willingness to participate in that flexibility of space usage resulting in a ministry which is best for the total church. (One implication of this is that child-sized bathroom fixtures hamper such full flexibility. While such specialized fixtures may be required by some states for day care programs and are a favorite of many children's teachers, few public buildings or homes have them.)

Another possibility for multipurpose use is the open classroom concept. Public schools have had considerable experience in this area, some being more successful than others. Before either adopting or rejecting this option, interview the teachers from at least two churches which have open classrooms. Proper design, adequate equipment plus good visual and acoustical control are essentials for a beneficial experience. Storage cabinets on wheels can establish boundaries for the activity of each class and provide visual control as well as space for books, consumable supplies, and other items. Chalkboards, tackboards, and even acoustical tiles can be attached to the back and sides of the storage cabinets depending upon the need. Portable panels to divide spaces are also available in many functional, attractive styles. Movable cabinets or panels may be constructed economically by church members themselves. Carpeting and acoustical ceilings are essential for such space. When it works satisfactorily, the open classroom allows much flexibility both in the ministry of teaching and in the use of that space for other, compatible programs.

Some congregations are providing Christian education classes after school instead of, or as a supplement to, Sunday classes. In either case, a longer time is available for education, and thus the classrooms are used more often. In certain communities, another opportunity for greater utilization of space is a released time program during the school day for religious training. All such options deserve investigation so that facilities may be flexible enough to meet the needs if the congregation desires to participate in these programs. Whatever degree of multi-use is possible, educational spaces should be equipped with adequate wiring capacity and sufficient electrical outlets to allow a variety of contemporary teaching techniques.

Flexible space can well serve all areas of church life. Rooms designed for single use are costly both initially and throughout their useful lives. There is no theological case against multi-use space. The inconveniences are few and the benefits are many. Wise stewardship demands that both new and existing church structures greatly increase their proportion of flexible space.

Conserving Energy 4

As this chapter is being written, millions of people still doubt that there is a serious, worldwide energy problem. Such lack of awareness persists in spite of many reports of shortages and stories about the higher costs that always accompany shortages. A newspaper article has stated "cost of utilities at the largest Baptist Church in the world are expected to climb to *more than $1,000 a day by 1981.*" The 1973 utility bill for this church was $100,000. By 1976 it had doubled. Without decreasing use of the building, utility costs are conservatively estimated to be almost $400,000 by 1981.

While changes in the past decade regarding energy resources and costs have been enormous, they are only part of the rapidly increasing whirlpool in which much of humanity finds itself. Norman Cousins warns us of the danger: "Ultimately, the acceleration (of change) produces irreverence. Men in increasing motion cover ground but have none to stand on. Values take on a free-floating quality. . . . it is not just a matter of rejecting values; it is a matter of being disconnected from the things that give rise to values."[1] In spite of such grave potential consequences, escape from change seems impossible.

Futurists predict no respite from the current dilemma. Here is a representative sample:

> More and more people and less and less food, energy, water, and of nearly all other resources per person; growing awareness of precarious-

[1] Norman Cousins, *The Nature of a Humane Society* (Philadelphia: Fortress Press, 1976), p. 190. Used with permission of the publisher.

ness of life; increasing sense of global interdependence; affluence, gracious living possible for fewer people. Responses to these changes range from withdrawal to sacrificial sharing.

Continued loss of confidence in the ability of institutions to solve crucial problems as the pace of change and increasing complexity outstrip resources and abilities of institutions to adapt and cope.[2]

Contemporary prophets have forecast shortages of energy resources, but as with their predecessors, the general public has not taken them seriously. The only thing sudden about the energy shortage is the preoccupation with it. Economists, ecologists, scientists, and various other specialists have been giving warnings for years that precious natural resources were being spent as though there would be no tomorrow. Now, like it or not, tomorrow is here. In the 1950s the Paley Report, commissioned by President Truman, predicted a severe shortage of oil. In 1970, John A. Carver, Jr., member of the Federal Power Commission, said: "A crisis exists right now. For the next three decades we will be in a race for our lives to meet our energy needs."

The basic cause of the problem has been overconsumption of a relatively inexpensive product. This has been particularly true of the United States where, with only 6 percent of the world's population, one-third of the world's energy is consumed. As an example of this general lack of concern for energy use, the design of church buildings has seldom taken energy conservation seriously into account. The assumption has been that whatever space is constructed can be heated and cooled by fossil fuels (gas, coal, oil) to a satisfactory level of human comfort. This assumption is no longer valid. As many congregations are discovering, the cost of utilities is now becoming prohibitive.

There are those who say that, given necessary profit incentives, oil companies and others in the energy production field will be able to meet the demand indefinitely. The prestigious *Wall Street Journal* presented this thesis in its May 27, 1977, edition, which included examples of previous resource predictions that proved to be extremely inaccurate on the low side.[3] But even if there should happen to be much more oil and natural gas than most scientists estimate or if nuclear fusion should become practical on a large scale,

[2] Douglas A. Walrath, from an article in *New Conversations* (Fall-Winter, 1976), p. 6. Used with permission from the author.
[3] *Wall Street Journal*, May 27, 1977.

the problems of cost, pollution, and just distribution still remain. Conservative projections of future utilities price increases are around 10 percent per year. Other estimates range as high as 20 percent. It appears as if prices will continue to increase substantially whether it is from dwindling supplies or the greatly increased cost of digging and drilling deeper for fossil fuels that may or may not even be there.

What happens to the environment must also be a great concern for Christians. There is evidence that the earth cannot stand the air and water pollution which are inevitable side effects of a high energy-use society. As R. Buckminster Fuller has said, "The universe is not going to tolerate our preposterous ego in playing the short-sighted game of exploitation we've been playing."[4] Widespread change to a more simple life-style would be beneficial to the planet and also, probably, to the individual.

An unusual prophet and architect, Malcolm Wells, has beautifully explained the steps in the energy cycle:

> Last year, somewhere in Florida, on the leaves of a forgotten sugar-cane plant, a bit of sunlight ended its eight-minute dash to earth. Somehow, the plant turned that sunlight into sugar. Somehow, the sugar got into my sugarbowl and then into my morning coffee. I sipped last year's sunshine at breakfast. Now it's in my blood, and it starts to feed these old architect-muscles. It's dark now, and I start for home. My muscled sunlight suddenly becomes pedal-power, then chain-pull, wheel-spin, generator-whine, filament-heat and finally—from the headlamp—light again! Miracle![5]

Such a miracle takes on even more meaning when one is personally involved in using a simple, inexpensive, nonpolluting bicycle for transportation.

While all predictions about the future are subject to error, what has already been happening in regard to high-cost energy consumption is alarming enough. A church in New York had to reduce its staff because of the high winter heating bill. A church in West Virginia was told before construction began that its new building would cost $200 a month to heat with electricity. By the time the building was completed, the bill was well over $500 per month. Another church discovered that it was paying $8,000 a year for energy and maintenance due to rising costs in these areas. The least that is likely

---

[4] Philadelphia *Bulletin*, August 28, 1977, Sec. 4, p. 2.
[5] Malcolm Wells, *Energy Essays* (Barrington, N.J.: Edmund Scientific Co., 1976), p. 26. Used with permission of the publisher.

to happen in coming years is continually increasing costs for energy and periodical shortages that could be very widespread.

A reduction of energy usage is thus recommended not only based upon supply and cost factors but also because conservation is Christian. Reflection upon the entrance of humankind into what has been called the "age of scarcity" finds two Christian teachings converging: God as the Creator of everything and stewardship as a central element in the life of the church and its members. All material resources are gifts from God to be used wisely, not squandered in a selfish manner. The Christian is never justified in using more resources than is necessary because of the effect of so doing on others.

> If, as appears likely, ecological limitations will restrict the continued exponential growth of industrial civilization, we will act responsibly. We will not say: "Let's use it up—God will provide more." Instead we will do what we can to enable our society to go through a very difficult period of transition from physical growth to dynamic equilibrium. Perhaps we will again begin to affirm a slogan of our ancestors: "Waste not, want not," and at the same time take steps to make sure that every person on this planet has his fair share of the world's limited resources.[6]

Conservation of energy supports the goals of the congregation because it frees a higher proportion of the budget to be used in direct ministries to people. Without taking prudent steps to reduce utility bills, budget allocations will inevitably increase for the "overhead" function of providing a church building. Thus, in a direct sense, reallocation supports ministry. More time, energy, and money can be devoted to caring programs which demonstrate Christian love.

How can conservation be accomplished? Specific steps may be taken with both existing buildings and new construction.

Existing Church Buildings

The first step is to have a thorough "energy checkup" of the building. This can be done by a mechanical engineer, contractor, or the church trustees. For a large structure, the fee paid to an engineer would probably be a wise investment. The service might include such procedures as checking the efficiency of the heating–air-conditioning systems, determining the heat loss of the building, and making specific recommendations for improvement. Fuel consumption for the last five years should be reviewed.

[6] Owen Owens, "Stewardship in a Transitional Era," an unpublished paper, p. 4. Used with permission.

A self-study could include inspection of the heating system, air infiltration at doors and windows, the amount of insulation in walls and ceilings, thermostat settings maintained, and the use of rooms for various meetings. Here are some simple energy conservation tips:

1. Make sure oil and gas burners are cleaned, adjusted, and serviced once each year. Furnace filters should be cleaned or changed regularly. Gas burner pilot lights can be turned off during the summer months. Better yet, install a self-igniting pilot that operates only when the thermostat calls for heat from the furnace.

2. Seal the building as tightly as possible. This is the simplest and least expensive way for any church to reduce its fuel consumption. Wind penetration and the loss of heat through cracks, porous walls, the roof, unsealed doors and windows, etc., add considerable cost to the utility bill. For example, a poorly fitted sash window without weather stripping will admit five times as much air as a weather-stripped window which fits well. Procedures to decrease heat loss usually pay for themselves in a few years. These include weather stripping around doors, using strong door closers, caulking around window and door frames and any other places where air leaks occur, and adding storm windows and storm doors to all doors and windows that are exposed to the exterior, including stained-glass windows.

3. Adjust thermostats so that heat will be used only when and where it is needed. Spaces can be maintained at 55 degrees or less between uses. Supply colorful, warm afghans for use in the sanctuary for those who feel the cold more. The entire worship space does not need to be maintained at a relatively high temperature all week just to benefit the organ. Check with the organ manufacturer for advice about isolating the instrument and recommended temperature and humidity conditions. If it is possible and feasible, consider dividing the building into smaller heating zones so that a large furnace does not need to work to heat only a portion of the building, such as the offices, meeting rooms, or day care center.

4. Arrange meeting schedules to save fuel. Some churches now hold all board meetings on one night, with child care available for families who have both parents involved. Consider meeting in homes, which are already being heated.

5. If the church has the option and it is judged to be feasible, switch to the cheapest, most efficient heating fuel. Electricity normally costs two or three times as much per thermal unit as oil. An oil burner can be up to 75 percent efficient while electricity furnishes only 30 percent of the energy that was used to generate it at the power plant. If electricity is used, heat pumps have higher efficiency than radiant heating systems.

6. Add insulation to the walls, ceiling, and also under the floor if there is a crawl space. Most church buildings need at least twice as much insulation as was installed during construction. As a general rule, it is economically feasible for buildings in the middle and northern states to have 12 inches of standard fiber glass insulation above the ceilings and 6 inches in the walls. An engineer or qualified heating contractor should know the insulation requirement of the region. Insulation materials are rated with an "R" value. This value measures heat resistance. A higher "R" value indicates greater resistance to heat loss. In central and northern Michigan, for example, R-38 is recommended for ceilings. Two six-inch fiberglass batts have a value of 38. In Kansas, R-30 is suggested, which is equivalent to $9\frac{1}{2}$ inches of fiberglass. There are several other types of insulation, such as solid panels, foam, and loose fill. Most churches will be able to find insulation in a form that can be used for their particular structure and design. Adequate insulation will normally pay for itself in fuel saving within three or four years. At the present rate of inflation for fuel, $1 saved now will amount to nearly $16 worth of savings in just 10 years.

7. One other possibility is the provision of double doors with air locks at all entrances, especially those on the north and west sides of the building. When services and meetings are held, doors may be left open long enough to allow considerable heat loss. If there are two sets of doors with sufficient space between them to allow one to be shut before the other opens, a high percentage of air infiltration will be stopped.

Any church can determine the Energy Efficiency Ratio (EER) of its building fairly easily. The EER represents the amount of heat required for each cubic foot of building space in response to the severity of outside temperatures. It is not a scientific measurement of heat loss, but rather a relative indication of the thermal efficiency of a building and the degree of corrective action that may need to be taken. The method for figuring the EER will be found in Appendix B.

The lower the EER, the more efficient is the building. Limited experience with the formula thus far reveals that an EER of 1.3 indicates an efficient building in which heat loss has been reduced by various of the methods recommended. An EER between 1.3 and 1.7 would be average and indicates some corrective measures should be taken, such as reducing thermostat settings, adding storm windows, weather stripping, and insulation. An EER of over 1.7 would indicate inefficient energy usage and would require, in addition to the foregoing, major remedies such as the repair or replacement of the entire heating system, addition of double doors and considerably more insulation in walls and ceilings.

In the fall of 1977, United Methodists, United Presbyterians, and American Baptists sponsored Energy Conservation Analyses of three church buildings in Springfield, Massachusetts. The results were presented to a conference by the consulting professionals from Total Environmental Action, Incorporated.[7] The study indicated the following steps to be most cost-beneficial for reducing fuel consumption in existing church buildings (see Appendix C for a checklist of fuel saving measures.):

1. Reduce the demand by setting thermostats at 55 degrees in all spaces at night and whenever they are not being used. If the building does not have several controlled zones, the provision of separate heaters for such areas as offices is often more logical than heating an entire structure for a few people. A heating contractor is required to effect changes in the heat distribution system. With thermostat setbacks, sufficient time needs to be allowed to warm spaces before people arrive. For years, people have not adjusted thermostats because the cost of fuel was so low that the savings didn't make the effort seem worthwhile. Recent cost increases and various studies now seem to be changing public opinion on this subject. In the Springfield study, reduced thermostat settings had the highest benefit/cost ratio in two of the churches and came in fourth from the top for the third church. In that church, however, the most beneficial change was also in this category of reduced demand. It was found that an exhaust fan operated more than was necessary, carrying heat outdoors. Reducing the use of this fan to necessary occasions was

[7] See *Energy Stewardship*, a paper prepared by Total Environmental Action, Inc., Harrisville, New Hampshire 03450. See Appendix C of this book for a "Check List for Reducing Fuel Use in Church Buildings."

estimated to save 19 percent on fuel bills. Automatic timers may be used so the building can warm up ahead of time.

2. Reduce heating system fuel waste by keeping the furnace running at peak efficiency and minimizing loss in the distribution system. Regular maintenance of the furnace and repair or replacement of worn parts is important. A motorized stack damper was recommended for each church. This damper blocks the loss of heat up the chimney by automatically closing when the burner is not operating. (While some building codes do not allow stack dampers, changes in technology and wider acceptance may come in the future. If a damper is to be used, care must be taken that it meets all local fire and safety codes.) In circulating water or steam systems, air pockets or improperly maintained steam traps can reduce efficiency and should be corrected. If hot water pipes or air ducts pass through unheated areas, such as a crawl space under the floor, wrapping with insulation will reduce heat loss.

3. Reduce the heating load by sealing up the building. This includes such items as insulation, storm windows, weather stripping, and caulking. In one of the churches, the adding of insulation in the ceiling was second in cost benefits; it ranked third in another of the church buildings studied. If the place needing insulation is not easily accessible, the expense of installation can rapidly decrease the cost/benefit ratio. For large sanctuary windows, removable interior insulating shutters were recommended as possibilities for two churches. These can be made of two-inch thick foam rubber covered with a water-resistant fabric and held in place by friction. (There is some fire hazard associated with these materials that needs to be reviewed thoroughly.) Protection from winter winds by evergreen trees and bushes reduces cold air infiltration.

The research for these three churches included a figure showing the long-term financial advantage of each suggested step. For example, in one building the adding of roof insulation was estimated to save $12 over a 35-year period for each dollar spent now. The decision to spend this money may simply be a businesslike decision involving a good return on investment, but churches are less accustomed than businesses to thinking in these terms. These savings can also be thought of as money the church will have in the future to put to other uses and as resources which are being conserved for future generations.

Some state and federal government programs now give a

financial incentive for taking energy conservation measures. Without that, however, there is still strong financial motivation in terms of reduced future fuel bills. For the church, there is the added satisfaction which comes from being good stewards of God's creation. Steps that will make a difference can be taken now with existing buildings.

New Construction

Based upon the knowledge now available about pollution and future fuel supplies, energy conservation should be a requirement of the highest priority in the design of all structures, including church buildings. If facility improvements are necessary, the thoughtful congregation will plan carefully and write out its program goals as suggested in chapter 1. Energy conservation ought to be an explicit, integral part of each goal that has facility implications. The anticipated building should utilize conservation measures that are cost effective, resulting in decreased use of nonrenewable energy resources and increased use of alternate, renewable resources.

When the church has voted for facility improvements incorporating minimal energy usage, the next step is to select an architectural firm which is aware of this urgent need and knows the most recent technical advances in the field. This may not be an easy task. Many architects and engineers are not yet as aware as they could be of energy criteria which impact upon building design, the selection of mechanical systems, construction materials, site factors, and building orientation. Architects have enjoyed a period of few questions and general disinterest in energy conservation. Financial institutions have emphasized low initial costs and ignored the impact of long-term costs. The majority of architects, along with most of the population, are still operating on the assumption that there is an unlimited supply of fossil fuels.

It is time for those who need the services of an architect to add another selection criterion to the favorites of programming, aesthetics, and good construction. Architects must now reeducate themselves regarding energy issues. New tools for conservation and the use of alternate, renewable sources of energy must be evident in the design portfolio of a relevant architect.

Energy Conservation Factors

The first and most important energy factor to analyze is the planning skill of an architect. Some architects are quick to proclaim how many church buildings they have designed. Quite often an examination of the end product illustrates the repetition of antiquated concepts of single use and inflexible space. Some of this can be blamed upon rigid and unlearned clients. However, the majority can be pegged as the absence of coordinated design processes which domonstrate the integration of financial, programmatic, and aesthetic realities.

How does the architect's planning skill relate to energy conservation? The measure of energy use relates directly to the measure of program use. One design may produce one unit of program activity while another may produce ten units. Remember, an architect's fee is usually based on the construction cost of the building and not on the productivity of the space. When clients make productivity of space a criterion for architectural selection, more architects will demonstrate this skill. The use of available space planning concepts will result in more program possibilities in less space which requires less energy to be spent in the manufacture of building materials, less energy for climatic control and for the life maintenance of the building.

A second energy factor relates to the technical skills which should be evidenced in the completed work of an architect. When energy questions are raised with most architects, they begin to evade the issues by giving assurance that they use only the best mechanical engineers available. The truth is that most designs are created in the mind of the architect and committed to drawings before establishing any energy use goals with the engineer. One measure of the work of an architectural firm is on the basis of energy goals set and energy goals accomplished. When this kind of data is requested, architects will begin to recognize the need to reeducate themselves for the job of conserving energy and protecting their clients' cash flow for years to come.

The question "How do you determine how much insulation should be put in a building?" was asked of several architects. Not one satisfactory answer was received. All of the impacting factors such as weather and temperature data, cost of insulation, cost of energy, rate of interest, and the length of a mortgage have been incorporated into a formula which can be used by architects in designing and specifying insulation standards for buildings. Until these available technical skills become functional for architects, using a "competent" mechanical engineer will not protect the church against increasing future energy costs.

A third energy factor relates to a general knowledge of long-term trends and their effect on the ecological system. The architect must accept the challenge of evaluating and incorporating alternate sources of renewable energy. This includes a working knowledge of the availability and effectiveness of techniques and systems to be covered later in this chapter. An observer of successful projects develops a sense of disbelief when told by numerous architects that the use of solar energy is unfeasible. What they are saying is that they have not taken the time to study seriously the information and technology that are already available.

Heavy responsibility for changing energy patterns in building design rests with architects. However, as the potential clients who are interviewing architects, churches have power to influence this group of professionals and need to use that power.

When an architectural firm that is aware of energy concerns is selected, early discussion of the subject will touch several topics. If a new building is to be constructed, its orientation on the site will be extremely important. For decades now, the availability of relatively low-cost fuel has caused designers to ignore site factors, such as the angle of the sun, tree location, and prevailing winds. The assumption has been that an unlimited, cheap supply of energy could heat, cool, ventilate, and light the space however it was oriented. This assumption can no longer be followed.

There is a need to become familar again with site-orientation techniques known to past civilizations, including Indians in the Southwest. Centuries ago, they built their homes (adobe, earth bricks, or caves) in the location best suited to receive warm rays from the sun in the winter, shade and cooling breezes in the summer. This major assistance from nature reduced their need for fuel. Such simple techniques constitute, not a lost art, but one that has been ignored and now should be revived.

While solar energy for churches will be discussed in more detail in the next chapter, it should be mentioned here that one type of "passive" solar system simply requires locating the building so as to take advantage of free heat from the sun. In the winter, solar heat comes from three directions: East, West, and mainly from the South. However, this heat source cannot be tapped if there are no openings to allow the sun to come through or if the spaces that could benefit from such heat are not properly located within the building.

It takes little scientific expertise to know that rooms with large, south-facing windows are warmer in winter than any other rooms. This is because heat from the sun is absorbed by the floor, walls, and furniture, then radiates throughout the room. Good design and use of materials can take care of excess glare should that be a problem. A relatively small roof eave keeps out the high summer sun. Double- or triple-glazed windows allow the sun's warm rays to come through while providing adequate insulation against heat loss. For example, a double-glazed window reduces heat loss by 53 percent as compared to a single pane of glass while permitting 87 percent of the sun's rays to enter.

Much conventional wisdom about energy conservation advises that buildings should have as few windows as possible. While a well-insulated wall will retain more heat than a double-glazed window, that same wall does not permit the entrance of any light or heat from the sun. With adequate design, large south-facing windows or sliding-glass doors allow enough heat to enter to more than compensate for losses due to a lower insulation rating. The amount of heat retainage is enhanced by insulated drapes or shutters that may be used to cover the windows at night. There is only one-third as much heat loss with tight-fitting insulated shutters as without.

Another site-orientation factor is that there should be as little exposure as possible in the direction of prevailing winter winds, which for much of the United States is the north or northwest. If the site allows, an earth berm (small hill or shelf) could be located near the wall on the side of prevailing winter winds to send them up and over rather than directly at the building. Windows facing that direction should be kept to a minimum, and it would be best to have no major entrances on that side. If a major entrance is necessary on the side facing prevailing winter winds, double doors with an air lock are essential.

Evergreen trees located between the building and the direction of prevailing winter winds also reduce air infiltration. If this direction is northwest, as is common, tall trees will provide shade from the hot, late afternoon summer sun. Deciduous trees will not greatly reduce heat from the afternoon winter sun because there are no leaves at that time of year. A minimum of trees to the south and southwest will allow passage of cool summer breezes. The contours of the site and other nearby physical objects, including buildings, also need to be taken into account in orienting a new structure. Careful orientation according to the local climate and the uniqueness of the site has the potential of conserving much energy.

Another topic which the church and its architect will want to discuss thoroughly is the energy conservation implications of design and use of materials. Of particularly important concern for churches is the space used for worship. The extremely high sanctuary ceilings of medieval cathedrals were meant to say something about the greatness of God, the power of the church, and the upward direction from which humanity was to receive inspiration. However, this kind of worship room contains such a large volume of space that it is next to impossible to maintain a temperature conducive to prolonged, multipurpose use. In the winter, much of the heat rises toward the ceiling, warming only inaccessible space.

The desired symbolism may be provided apart from the church building by a free-standing cross or bell tower. Acceptance of this or some similar option allows design of worship space with sufficient vertical dimensions to accommodate the seating capacity, be adequate for good vision and acoustics, and be pleasing aesthetically while containing a minimum of overhead, unusable space. During the 1950s and 1960s, most church buildings seemed to be all roof with their peaks soaring to thirty or forty feet or more. Even if one thinks solely of energy conservation concerns, one hopes that the day of this type of design has passed.

Another relevant factor is the subject of exposed exterior walls. Two buildings with the same floor space may have a considerable difference in their exterior wall volume because of the way they were designed. With more walls exposed to the weather, there is increased potential of heat loss. The building shape which results in the least exterior wall area related to volume of floor space is a circle; the next most efficient shape is a square.

Probably the most inefficient design for cool climates is the "campus plan" which has separate buildings for each room or group of similar spaces. The different sections of the campus are connected by enclosed halls or covered walkways. While usually popular only in very mild climates because of air circulation advantages, this design is sometimes used in other regions where it often results in high heating bills. A multistoried building provides additional energy efficiency if its use is not compromised by such program factors as inaccessibility to the handicapped or inability of multipurpose spaces to relate well to each other. Provided that program needs and reasonable aesthetical values can be met, it is best to have the smallest possible exposed exterior wall area.

An energy-conserving design with significant potential is that of having the building partially or totally underground. Humankind probably first lived in caves, like the animals, for shelter from the elements and protection from enemies. For similar reasons, the early Christian church often met underground. In the province of Cappadocia, Turkey, there are over seventy decorated churches cut from subterranean rock. Underground structures are now being considered as a possible means of conserving fuel as well as requiring a smaller amount of building material. Fuel savings come because the large earth mass slows down temperature changes. While air temperature may range over 100 degrees in a year, temperatures change only a few degrees below the frost level. Thus, when properly designed and insulated, an underground structure acts as a storage system and retains heat for a relatively long period of time. Likewise, in the summer, temperatures tend to remain constant with little need for mechanical assistance. Obviously, energy usage is not the only cost factor. Some items will be higher, such as excavation, lighting, and ventilation; others will be lower, such as maintenance and fuel. Expenses can vary greatly, however, and the presence of too much water in the soil from a high water table can render such construction impractical.

Some building sites are sloped so that a structure partially underground is possible. This is especially attractive if the slope is in a southerly direction. Research has indicated some negative psychological reactions to an underground environment, mainly feelings of confinement and the lack of an outside view. However, others feel they can concentrate more on their tasks without visual distractions and some have created substitute "windows" from fish tanks, floral arrangements, or art work.

One acknowledged leader on the subject of underground structures and environmental preservation is Malcolm Wells, who says:

> The truth is that underground buildings—at least the kind most architects propose—are naturally sunny and bright. They open from the sides of hills or into sunken sun-gardens. Underground buildings do cost a little more than other buildings; after all, they have to carry the extra weight of those beautiful rooftop gardens. But they offer us a healthy

alternative to our dying cities of asphalt and concrete. Imagine, rooftop wild gardens downtown!

Underground buildings need very little outside maintenance and they offer excellent fire protection and storm-proofing. They're unbelievably quiet and—best of all—they save so much money in heating and cooling bills their extra costs get repaid often in less than ten years.

. . . there's really only one big reason to build this way. It is the very basis of life on our particular planet. Biologists tell us the life-scheme here is this: green plants covering the *entire surface* of this sun-bathed sphere, every inch that's not ice, desert, or rock. Our lives depend on it.

So why in the world do we build all our highways and buildings in the only way that is sure to destroy us?[8]

An underground elementary school has been in operation in New Mexico since 1962. Extensive studies indicate that there have been no adverse effects or increased anxiety on the part of students or faculty and that the community evidenced overwhelming support for and acceptance of the earth-covered school. In fact, there has been "a slight positive effect on the general physical and mental health of pupils. They were a bit calmer and seemed less prone to respiratory diseases" than students from the three other schools tested.[9] While underground construction shatters the image of a church building with a steeple on a hill, it may be far more practical for facing the demands of the future. It is at least worthy of some consideration.

The materials used in construction have direct implications for energy conservation. Where residential-type structures are possible, the use of 2″ x 6″ studs allows over 50 percent more insulation than the standard 2″ x 4″ size. Concrete blocks and bricks are poor insulators; so when used in walls, the design should provide for the insertion of rigid insulation. If the roof design will not accommodate 9 inches to 12 inches of fiber-glass insulation, space may be provided for other types giving a similar degree of resistance to the flow of heat. Most types of insulation require vapor barriers to keep them from deteriorating due to moisture condensation. In moderate to cold regions, insulation (such as Styrofoam) under concrete slab floors, around the slab perimeter, and on the outside surface of subgrade walls is beneficial.

Other energy conservation measures include weather stripping and caulking, adequate ventilation, provisions for changing humidity

[8] Wells, *op. cit.*, p. 64.

[9] Frank L. Moreland, ed., *The Use of Earth Covered Buildings* (U.S. Government Printing Office, 1976).

to optimum levels for the conditions, and insulating hot-water pipes and air ducts. Exterior doors may be steel with a urethane core and magnetic weather stripping. Heating and cooling equipment should be adequate but not oversized. The type of system should be chosen carefully with availability, long-term cost, flexibility, and energy conservation potential in mind. Dividing a building into several heating/cooling zones based upon the type and frequency of use will normally save energy and money. The cost of manual or electrical controls for zoning is usually small compared to potential fuel savings.

If possible, include windows that may be opened to provide ventilation. Public buildings with inoperable windows must provide mechanical ventilation whenever the space is occupied. Structures of all types have been built in recent decades with dozens or even thousands of inoperable windows. There are many days in the spring, summer, and fall during which moderate temperatures and light winds provide completely adequate natural ventilation. Those fresh breezes are also completely inaccessible if the windows will not open. So fan motors hum on, using 30 percent efficient electricity to move air that nature is moving free of charge. (Buildings in which smoking is not allowed may have reduced air circulation requirements.)

Economic Factors

As the congregation evaluates various energy conservation possibilities, pay-back periods must be compared in order to make a fair judgment. If the funds to meet the initial cost are on hand or may be borrowed on reasonable terms, the question becomes, how many years will it take for fuel savings to equal the cost of the energy-conserving improvement? Suppose a proposal to add insulation and storm windows will cost the church $4,400 plus $600 interest on a three-year loan for a total of $5,000. Some members react negatively because that seems like a lot of money and, besides, it must be borrowed. Others support the proposal, feeling that fuel savings will equal the expenditure in a few years and, from that point on, the savings will mean that money can be changed to priority areas of the church budget. How can the congregation know if this expenditure is worthwhile?

While absolutely exact knowledge about future trends is impossible, there are sufficiently accurate projections available to deal with this question. Three figures placed in a formula will yield a reasonably accurate answer. First is the cost of the improvement (storm windows and insulation in this example) plus interest if a loan is required. Next is the amount of fuel savings anticipated during the first year after the improvement. This can be determined with reasonable accuracy by comparing the building heat loss before the improvement with that anticipated afterwards. A heating contractor or mechanical engineer can provide these figures. Finally, the average anticipated fuel inflation rate for the future is included. With these three figures available, the formula in Appendix D will give the number of years necessary for building improvements or items included in a new structure to pay for themselves. The example found in Appendix D indicates that a $5,000 expenditure on insulation and storm windows with an anticipated annual inflation rate of 10 percent will pay for itself in approximately eight years.

Initial cost can no longer be the major criteria for deciding whether or not to add insulation, build partially underground, or install a solar heating system. Data about costs which take fuel scarcity and escalating inflation seriously should be an essential part of reaching such decisions.

Solar Energy for Churches 5

The events of recent history relating to the availability of fuels have taught an important lesson which should not be lost. It is advantageous to have a backup energy system for any building. A furnace or boiler that has separate burners and supply systems which allow the use of either oil or gas will continue to operate even if one of these fuels is temporarily cut off. A self-contained diesel or gasoline generator can be utilized during brief electrical outages. If the system may be adjusted and enough storage space is available, a backup coal-fired boiler might be an option worthy of consideration by larger churches. Relatively large supplies of coal appear to be available. The church that has the capability of switching to a second fuel source will be prepared for some of the kinds of shortages that have already been experienced.

When both the main and backup systems rely upon fossil fuels, however, there is still a long-range risk factor because of the limited supply of oil, gas, and coal contained in the earth. Thus, the search is on for workable and cost-feasible alternative energy from such sources as the sun, wind, tides, and geothermal geysers. While nuclear fission may increase in importance, problems relating to potential atomic warfare, safety, pollution, and waste disposal leave that energy source in doubt for the present. Nuclear fusion sounds like the ideal solution, but it could be many years from practical use. For the coming decades (and perhaps far beyond), solar heat seems to be the most likely alternative energy source.

"Professor E. S. Morse of the Essex Institute has devised an ingenious arrangement for utilizing the sun's rays in warming our houses; it consists of a surface of blackened slate under glass fixed to the sunny side of a house. The thing is so simple and apparently self-evident that one only wonders that it has not always been in use." This quotation is not from the latest edition, but rather appeared in the *Scientific American* magazine of May 13, 1882! Solar heating is a basically simple ideal, and it has been known about for a long time. Furthermore, solar energy has been used in numerous installations during this century. However, a warning must be given that real expertise is still needed if this option is being considered by the church.

Recent experience indicates that two quick reactions to solar energy are common. One is the statement that a particular part of the country has too many cloudy days each year. The solar radiation which arrives at the earth's surface is called insolation. While the average insolation on a December day in Phoenix, Arizona, will be twice that in Portland, Maine, still, enough sunlight reaches the northeastern United States to make solar energy workable with the right equipment.

The average number of sunny hours in various parts of the country can be expressed as a percentage of the approximately 4,400 hours of total sunlight which is the theoretical maximum for much of the United States. Reports from 123 of the weather stations in the continental United States show only 13 where the mean percentage of annual sunlight is under 50%, with the lowest being 40%. Seventy of the stations (57%) receive an average of over 60% annual sunlight. Charts are available showing the average percentage of possible sunlight received for each month of the year. As an example, the lowest average number of sunny hours received during the year in Lincoln, Nebraska, is 55% during December. Weather records there for over 50 years reveal that 64% of possible annual sunlight has been received.

The intensity of sunlight reaching the earth is approximately 300 Btu's (British Thermal Units) every hour for each square foot of space. The insolation does not drop to zero on a cloudy day. In fact, solar collectors can continue operating if the cloud layer is not too thick. Because of cost and design considerations, solar heat will seldom meet 100% of the heating needs of a building. However, solar heat can be used in relationship to a fossil fuel system by providing 40%, 50%, 60%, or even more of the total heat required. Thus, solar energy usage is a practical possibility almost anywhere in the United States provided that a system is chosen which matches the needs of the particular area and has an economically feasible pay-back period.

The other quick reaction to solar energy is too quick an acceptance of its use without thorough investigation. There are already those who have moved to a decision too rapidly and have later regretted it. Some outstanding professionals in the field fear that eventual full acceptance of solar technology may be retarded by those who promise more than they can deliver. Most advertisements of the ever-increasing number of solar equipment manufacturers make it sound too simple. Therefore, it is essential to raise a number of key questions.

Is the building occupied enough hours per week to justify a solar installation? Has the building first been insulated and sealed as tightly as possible? What is the realistic estimated pay-back period? Which type of solar system should be considered? How will solar energy tie in with the present heating system? Is it easy to switch systems when a backup is needed? Is there a knowledgeable, experienced installer of solar heating nearby? What guarantees are provided by the installer and equipment manufacturer? Where will the storage system be located? For how many cloudy days will the storage capacity provide heat? How can the system be installed so that servicing and replacement of solar collectors is not an expensive or even impossible operation?

When a church raises the preceding questions, the answers may indicate that solar heat is not a practical alternative. On the other hand, they may point toward the feasibility of some type of installation. If so, it will be essential to separate myth from fact about this energy alternative which is really in its early stages of development so far as mass application is concerned.

Types of Solar Heating Systems

As engineers and inventors work at simplifying systems and reducing costs, two main types of systems have emerged. The simpler of these is the passive or direct system which has few, if any, moving parts. In effect, the passive system makes the building itself the solar collector through the use of large south-facing windows and increased mass, such as masonry walls, floors, or stored water within the building. This mass, which stores the sun's energy during sunny hours, reradiates heat during the cooler cycle at night. The illustration below represents one of many possible examples using glass and interior mass to collect and store heat.

The other type of solar heating system is called the active system and consists of three elements. These are a flat plate collector of either air or fluid type, a storage system, and a distribution system. A bin full of fist-sized rocks is used for air storage, while insulated tanks are used for water storage. If the water system does not drain down at night, some type of corrosion-resistant antifreeze must be used. Sometimes a heat exchanger is required to transfer heated air to a water system or vice versa. In the active system, the collectors can be attached to the building or be located very near the building. The illustration on the next page shows how the active solar system operates.

When a new building is to be constructed, as much passive solar heat collection as possible should be included in the design. Most new buildings can be designed and situated on the site to take some advantage of solar energy for space heating needs. This plus heavy insulation will reduce the requirement for an active solar system and fossil fuels. (Presently, solar air-conditioning is of questionable feasibility, although manufacturers are claiming improvements to

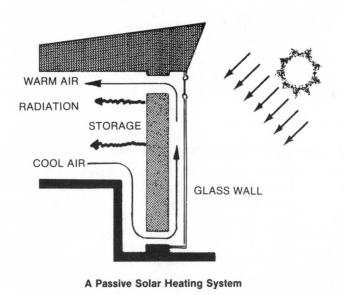

A Passive Solar Heating System

Diagram by American Baptist Extension Corporation

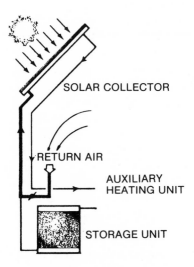

An Active Solar Heating System

overcome dependability and cost problems. Also, churches do not usually use enough "domestic" hot water to make that application practical.)

In an existing structure, however, it is often difficult to make changes so that there is any passive solar collection capacity. Usually, the position of the building on the site, location of windows, and structural elements prevent the kind of alterations necessary for receiving and storing direct solar radiation. Sometimes the building orientation and design make it possible to install an active water or air system on an existing structure. For efficient operation, special attention must be given to the way the solar system will function in relationship to the present heating system and the location of the necessary storage capacity.

For most existing buildings, the addition of insulation, storm windows, and a backup heater are more feasible than installing ("retrofitting") a solar energy system. To be cost-effective for most structures, an active solar system should meet a minimum of around 40 percent of the space heating needs. A professional analysis should be made to determine what combination of collector size and storage capacity is economically feasible. Current experience indicates that feasibility decreases rapidly when an active solar system is designed to provide more than 80 percent of the space heating requirements.

Solar Design Factors

When solar heating is planned for a new building, the design needs to reflect both energy conservation and aesthetic concerns. Conservation motives can be easily forgotten if the appearance is not reasonably pleasing. To strike a needed balance, some architects have made logical concessions. For example, in one community, the ideal angle for rooftop solar collectors is 54 degrees. That angle results in a steep, expensive, rather unattractive roofline. So, the architect designed a 45-degree angle roof which was more pleasing in appearance and decreased the collectible solar energy by less than 10 percent. In most designs, some compromises will need to be made so that both energy conservation concerns and a sense of attractiveness may be preserved.

Another design factor is the location of the storage system. The water tank or rock bed should be well insulated so that heat losses are kept to a minimum. If the building has a basement, some space there away from an outside wall would be good. Storage on higher floor levels requires extra support because of the heavy weight of the water or rocks. Sometimes underground storage is feasible if soil conditions or subterranean streams do not cause problems. The length of water pipes or air ducts to and from storage should be as short as possible to reduce heat losses.

Solar collectors usually have glass or some type of plastic cover. Some covers are susceptible to breakage and, therefore, their location is important. Because of the task they are to perform, solar collectors are often placed in elevated locations. Accessibility should be limited to those who will be needed for service work. Most collectors are glazed either with tempered glass or fiberglass-reinforced plastic in order to resist breakage. While susceptibility to breakage cannot be ignored, it is not the major factor that some at first surmise. A large array of solar collectors located at ground level near a school athletic field had an extremely low breakage record over several years.

If an active system is to be used, still another design factor is the required strength of supporting walls and the roof. Not only the weight of the collectors themselves must be considered, but also that of the heat transfer medium. If this is water, substantial additional weight may be involved. The cost of any necessary structural modifications to hold this weight should be included as part of the total cost of providing an active solar system.

While not universally accepted, there are several "rules of thumb" used relating to flat plate air or water solar collectors. One is that the solar collector area should be 25 to 35 percent of the building floor space to provide sufficient heat for a feasible operation. This assumes full occupancy of the building with the system providing 65 to 75 percent of the heat load. The climate, hours of occupancy, and storage capacity would obviously affect this general rule. For hot water storage, approximately 1.2 gallons is required for each square foot of collector area. In an air system, about one-half cubic foot of rock storage is needed for each square foot of solar collector. It should be recognized that specific conditions of particular installations may substantially alter these calculations.

To determine the feasibility of solar heat for church building design, the pay-back period of the system, including inflation, should be determined. (See Appendix C for the formula.) At least one church has included solar heat as an alternate in the bidding process. This means that architectural and engineering plans were included for a separate bid on the solar system. The general contract covered basic structural, electrical, and plumbing work so that the system could be installed later, if desired. The costs for this work, plus an extra architectural fee for preparing the alternate bid, were considered acceptable risks by the church to determine whether it could afford the solar installation at the time of construction. This procedure allows decisions to be made based on actual bids rather than just estimates.

It is not the intention of this chapter to go into great detail concerning the many factors involved in the use of alternative energy sources such as solar. Those interested are referred to the bibliography for further, in-depth resources on this subject.

Three Solar Heated Churches

This chapter will conclude with some information about three solar heated churches to illustrate that this alternate energy source is already being used. The needs of the congregations are very different. At the time of writing, one of the buildings has been occupied; one is either in late design stages or under construction; and the third was an architectural graduate school thesis project, some portions of which may be included in the final design of a church building on the East

Coast. The facts have been provided by the architect, engineer, and/or pastor involved. Full information is not available in every case. However, it is hoped that enough facts and basic concepts are included to assist the interested reader.

Center of Hope Church, Westminster, Colorado

This may have been the first solar-heated church building in the country. The system was installed in the new structure in the fall of

Photograph by George Ward, Denver, Colorado

Center of Hope Church, Westminster, Colorado

1976. Three building design factors were significant for energy conservation. First, there is maximum insulation. In the walls, six inches of fiberglass plus one-half inch of foam were used. The heat resistance totals R-24. In the roof, three inches of foam provides an R-30 insulation barrier. Second, the heating system was designed so that 65 percent of the heat that is in the ventilation air exhausted from the building is transferred to the incoming fresh air. This procedure reduces substantially the heating load requirement of the building. Third, the heating system is based on control of several zones. When the day-care center is in operation, for example, the temperature is maintained at 70 degrees there while the rest of the building is at 55 degrees. The use of a night thermostat and a 7-day time clock allow an automatic 15-degree setback at night. Such selective temperature settings further reduce the heat load. All three of these procedures may be followed in the design of any new structure and also in many existing buildings. They are a necessary part of the steps required for reducing the heat load to a point where solar becomes feasible.

The Westminster Church solar-heating system services 20,000 square feet of space, including a 2,000 square foot parsonage, and also provides 200 gallons of domestic hot water per day. An unusual feature is that the backup system, an electrical heat pump, is even solar assisted. Electrical energy is utilized to power fans, water pumps, and the heat pump. Designed into the roof (see picture) are all-copper water solar collectors covering a net area of 2,728 square feet. Of the total energy requirements, 86½ percent are provided directly from the solar collectors and 12½ percent from the solar-assisted heat pump.

To prevent freezing, the water from the collectors drains back into storage tanks when the system is not operating. The water temperature varies from 95 degrees up to 185 degrees. Two storage tanks have a total capacity of 14,000 gallons. Any excess heat is used for the parsonage. While the pastor's home has its own electrical backup system capable of meeting the total need, it has been calculated that usage should be limited to the coldest months of December and January. Even then, the engineers estimate that electricity should be needed for only about one-third of the heating requirement. Rather sophisticated controls, including a mini-computer and pneumatic thermostats, regulate the system.

The pastor says, "There are no disadvantages of any kind. We have encountered no major problems. We would do the same thing again. We just had a good opportunity to have a major solar system and did it because it was good business. We worried quite a bit about how it would work, but it works fine. We are excited about it, but the newness wears off."

The cost of the solar system was approximately $80,000. The engineers have estimated that with all factors considered, such as inflation and interest, all deficits will be overcome by the sixteenth year and the system will pay for itself by the twenty-third year. The engineers realize that this is a fairly long pay-back period but feel that it is one of the economic drawbacks of providing a system that covers such a large portion of the heating load. During the severe 1976—1977 winter, the estimated total heating bill for the church and parsonage was $797.75.

The pastor of the Center of Hope Church is Rev. Al Haan; the architect was J. K. Abrams; the solar system was provided by R-M Products Company, Don Erickson, engineer; the general contractor was E. M. Tamminga.

Church of the Valley, San Ramon, California

In designing for conservation, the architects of this church concentrated on three major areas of energy consumption: space heating, cooling and ventilation, and lighting. Because of the flexibility of the building program, the size of the site (5 acres), and

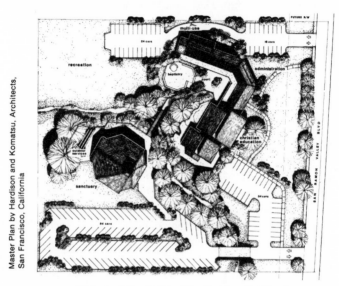

Church of the Valley, San Ramon, California

the relatively mild climate, a wide range of solutions to each of the three energy problems developed. In general, the approach involved architectural solutions wherever possible, leaving mechanical solutions to be used only where necessary. The final analyses showed that the church's original goal of a 75 percent reduction in conventional energy consumption was met and surpassed largely by architectural measures, with the solar system and a few other mechanical solutions making an important but relatively small contribution.

Space Heating

The solution to the problem of space heating depended heavily on envelope conservation of heat. Insulation standards were exceeded with the walls rated at R-23 and the roof R-28. Double glazing was used throughout, with weather stripping and door seals at all exterior openings. Contrary to standard practice for the climate, the slab edges were insulated. In addition, most of the grade level glazing was oriented to the south, with shading devices carefully designed to admit most of the desired winter sun. Such architectural measures are generally maintenance free.

Church of the Valley, Solar Collectors

Solid state controls will be programmed to anticipate the schedule of occupancy and to shut down the mechanical equipment when it is not needed. They will also control the amount of fresh air admitted to the system to meet, but not substantially exceed, the occupants' changing ventilation requirements.

The solar system was designed to provide 55 percent of the project's annual heating requirements with only 714 square feet of collectors. This is equal to 12 percent of the floor area of 6,080 square feet. It is estimated that these collectors will provide approximately 75 million Btu's of usable heat per year. Backup heat will be provided by high efficiency (80%) natural gas furnaces. Natural gas is still cheap and available in California at this writing, although the church is prepared to substitute a heat pump if the price or supply of gas should change. The solar system cost is approximately $27,500 of a $280,000 structure. The solar system estimated pay-back period is fifteen years.

The solar system is a drain-down water system, providing space heat and natural cooling. The copper flat plate collectors are single glazed and the absorber surface has a selective black coating for greater efficiency. The storage system includes two 550-gallon tanks. There will be two rows of 17 collectors each.

Church of the Valley, Natural Ventilation

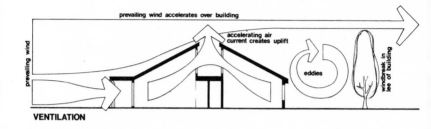

VENTILATION

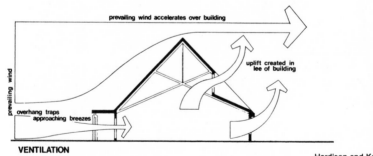

VENTILATION

Hardison and Komatsu

Church of the Valley, Use of Solar Energy

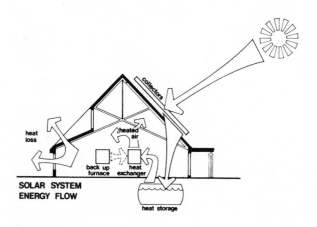

SOLAR SYSTEM
ENERGY FLOW

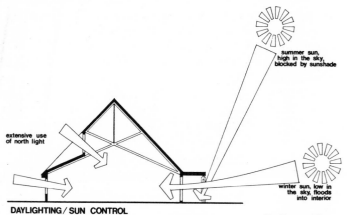

DAYLIGHTING / SUN CONTROL

Hardison and Komatsu

Cooling

As was the case with space heating, the solution to the cooling problem depended heavily on reducing load. South-facing glass is protected by deep overhangs, opaque for several feet and extended by trellises carrying deciduous vines. North and northeast facing glass is protected by vertical and horizontal shading devices. No glass faces east or west. The net effect of these measures is that the radiant heat gain through glass is essentially zero not only in the summer but also in the early autumn when the peak loads are encountered.

The control system will be programmed to enable the building to take advantage of the high daily temperature variations (typically 30 degrees) which prevail in this desert climate of hot dry days and cool nights. During the early morning hours when the outdoor air is at its coolest, the mechanical ventilation system will move outdoor air through the interior spaces, removing heat from the structure, enabling the heat buildup of the following day to be absorbed into the weight of the structure without raising the interior temperature above the comfort level. In the absence of the measures taken to reduce load, this system would not provide adequate cooling capacity; the combination of architectural and mechanical measures has enabled the designers of the project to avoid the use of mechanical refrigeration altogether, at considerable savings in both first and operating costs.

The prevailing breezes in this area are dependably (90%) from the southwest during the cooling season, and this is taken into account in the design for natural ventilation. The buildings are grouped around a courtyard which is open to the southwest to channel these breezes into the spaces where the radiant heat gain (from the afternoon sun) and the occupant load are the greatest.

Lighting

The general approach to the solution of the problem of lighting energy has been to maximize the use and usefulness of natural light and to use artificial lighting energy to maximum efficiency. First, natural light has been provided selectively, chiefly in the assembly and classroom spaces where it will be most appreciated. Second, the source of natural light has been placed to maximize its usefulness. Third, special switching systems have been provided to enable the level of artificial light change to respond to the changing level of natural light. Construction of this building began in February, 1978.

Pastor of the Church of the Valley is the Reverend Loren D. McBain. Architects are Hardison and Komatsu of San Francisco. The contractor is Jeff Orwig.

East Coast Church Building Design

In a recent thesis project, an architectural student designed a building in which the special needs involved in housing a congregation are brought into harmony with its surrounding environment. The basic concepts behind this new design may give some practical ideas to apply in planning for other energy-efficient structures. Features of this design could be incorporated in plans for buildings on other sites.

An unfathomable amount of the sun's energy constantly strikes the earth. This would amount to about 180 trillion kilowatts of electricity if it could be harnessed and utilized. Thus, a major goal of the thesis was to use some of this energy for heat by making the structure as energy efficient as possible. In order to make these energy concerns worthwhile in the context of the entire building, however, construction methods were to be kept as simple and inexpensive as possible.

With these goals in mind, necessary information was gathered regarding the site where the new building is to be located and the congregational program needs that must be satisfied. For energy conservation, the harmony between siting and programming is critical. Located in an urban setting, on the southern corner of a block, the southeast and southwest walls of the proposed building were designed to have as much glass area as possible to allow penetration of the sun's warm rays. The corresponding northeast and northwest walls have very few openings where heat may escape. Advantage was taken of the slope of the site to make these walls partially underground.

Because of the goal to keep the building and its systems simple, solar energy is used in a passive or direct approach in which the rooms themselves become collectors and storers of the energy. In the smaller rooms large amounts of glass on the southwest wall bring sunlight into the spaces and onto the concrete walls and floors. In the worship area, a large row of skylights admits the rays of the sun onto a large wall. The heat goes into the room as well as being absorbed by the wall. Insulation will be placed on the outside of the walls. With this design, the interior wall will give off heat until its temperature approximates that of the indoor air. This is the same principle that enables people to feel the warmth of a driveway pavement long after the sun has gone down.

Despite all the means by which this proposed building will receive heat from the sun, it is necessary to have a backup system to provide heat and air conditioning when the solar alone is not sufficient. Electric heat pump units will be used in this building. They will be console units located along the wall in the classroom section and large roof-mounted units over the sanctuary and narthex. These heat pump units are efficient and use few ducts and pipes so that their initial and continuing cost should be kept at a minimum.

As simple as such energy-saving measures may seem, they can produce significant results. It is estimated that 50 to 75 percent of the heat could be expected to come from the sun. In fact, the classrooms could well expect 100 percent of their heating needs to be supplied from the sun on most days, while the sanctuary would receive a lesser but still significant amount. This proposed building illustrates how low technology solutions and careful design can produce significant energy savings and thus good stewardship of God's resources.[1] (See illustrations for more details.)

[1] Information for this section has been supplied by Gary Sharp.

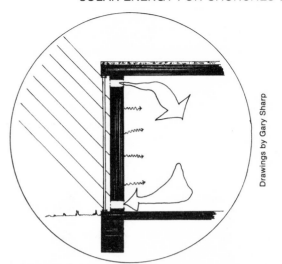

Drawings by Gary Sharp

This system, called a "Trombe Wall," allows sunlight to strike a concrete wall behind glass. The air heats up, rises, and enters the room while the cooler air near the floor is sucked into replace it. To cool the space, vents near the top could be opened to the outside to draw heat up and out.

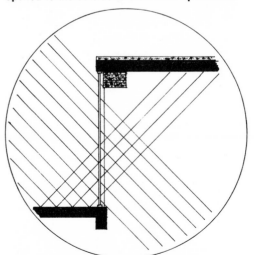

Glass windows, oriented toward the sun, can admit much of the sun's heat. This effect can be increased if a smooth, light-colored surface is outside to reflect more of the sun's rays through the windows.

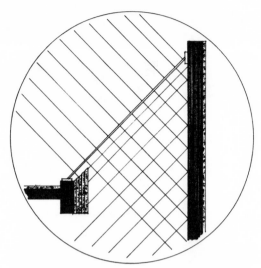

Skylights can directly admit solar energy while allowing for indirect lighting of interior spaces. Insulating shutters will reduce heat loss at night. In times when cooling is desired, vents at the top of the wall can exhaust warm air.

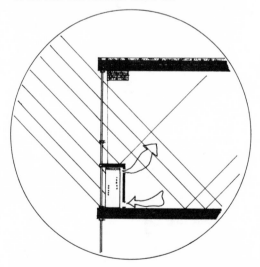

Water-filled cylinders can absorb twice as much heat as concrete; so the area under the sill height can be utilized to admit and store useful energy.

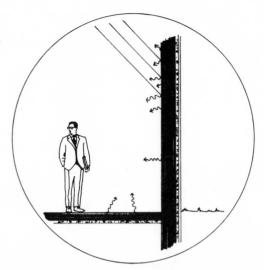

Insulation placed on the outside of the concrete walls, floors, and roof allows the concrete to absorb excess heat and store it until the room cools to the point where the heat is given back to the air. The concrete thus becomes a "heat sink" or heat storage mass.

Beautiful Church Buildings 6

The content of this chapter revolves around the meaning of one crucial word in its title. What appears beautiful to one person is not necessarily attractive to another. Beauty is in the eye of the beholder and is a very subjective topic. Therefore, it must be clear at the beginning that this discussion is about something much more than physical attractiveness. To emphasize this stance, no pictures of what a few individuals might consider beautiful church buildings will be included.

This is not to say that sterile design is recommended. To the contrary, if the following guidelines are incorporated, the result will be considered beautiful by many. Such beauty, however, must arise from the people involved and grow from the inside out. The dictionary definition of beauty supports the thesis that more than the physical is involved. Beauty "pleasurably exalts" not only the senses but also "the mind or spirit; physical, moral, or spiritual loveliness." This truth has been proven repeatedly.

Helen Keller rejoiced in the beauties of people and a world that she could neither hear nor see. Descriptions painstakingly communicated to her formed vivid pictures in her mind that were illuminated by her soul. Newspapers regularly report character and moral flaws of many so-called "beautiful people" of the world. Countless others, not blessed with physical attractiveness, lead quiet, saintly, beautiful lives.

Translated to church architecture, this philosophy implies that beautiful form follows relevant function "and faith precedes both." [1] If a design not only allows the congregation to carry out its mission but also enables and assists the effort, that design will be beautiful to those involved. A church building is not a monument to God, to the architect, or to the congregation which utilizes the space and pays the bills. Christians are workers with a very significant job to be accomplished, and the church building is a tool used by the workers in accomplishing their task. It is nothing more and nothing less than that.

Therefore, to achieve true beauty, the purposes and goals of the church should be reviewed before any designs are drawn. Ideally, ministry determines design rather than the reverse. The congregation that predetermines the style of architecture runs the risk of imprisoning itself and its program for several generations in a building that is often unsuited to its real mission. Architectural style ought not to be a point of departure, but rather the end result of honest and enlightened creative design to solve a particular building program. How much better to build around real needs than to squeeze or eliminate opportunities for mission just to fit a structure that might function beautifully someplace else or in some other generation!

Far too often, however, an unprepared building committee faces an overanxious architect. One such architect was known for his ability to whip out pencil and paper to draw several pretty sketches in the very first meeting. Another brought a completed model of his design to what was supposed to have been an initial interview. "Beautiful," said one committee member, "we'll take it." And they did! No discussion of belief, faith, purposes, goals, programs, or needs; no chance to allow the real function of the church to shape a design that could more accurately be called beautiful. Just an exterior shell, an idea which someone thought looked nice was thus imposed upon the congregation for fifty, seventy-five, or one hundred years. Such a procedure does not represent the beauty being advocated here. Consider, then, the following possibilities.

One guideline which may help a congregation to find its own way is the observation that beauty means simplicity and durability. Christians are taught to follow the example of their Master. Jesus was born in a barn and raised in a small, simple village. His vocation until

[1]Laurence H. Stookey, "Faith and Form," *Journal of the Guild for Religious Architecture* (Spring, 1976). Used with permission.

the age of thirty was that of carpenter. When starting his brief teaching and healing ministry, Jesus refused the offer to assume royal power or perform feats of magic. His companions were ordinary people, some of them social outcasts. He rejected legalism and imperialism. He elevated to prominence the most common elements, such as bread, water, and wine. His death came on a despised criminal's cross. Even after the resurrection, his appearance was so unspectacular that companions walking down a road did not recognize him.

Jesus summarized the 613 Hebrew commandments into love for God and for neighbor. This way of life has endured and grown through nearly two thousand years. It is a puzzling paradox how such a faith could ever spawn the ornate rituals, costumes, hierarchies, and buildings which too easily come to mind.

It needs to be recognized that Jesus allowed an expensive, extravagant gesture of love on at least one occasion during his earthly ministry. To show her devotion, a woman anointed his head with costly oil (Mark 14:3-9). To the surprise of the disciples, this rare act was praised, not condemned. The question for today is, how does the church demonstrate extravagant love for God? Because of the differences in people, there are many answers. It could be that an occasional demonstration of extravagance toward the church has its place. However, for most Christians, more satisfaction is received from giving to others than from spending on self. To be beautiful, a church building must be of a cost and design consistent with the way its owners wish to express their love for God and for people.

To say it in another way, for the Christian, beauty includes a theological element. If the congregation wants to emphasize in its ministry such subjects as humility or the superiority of love over material goods, it will be concerned about how its church building can echo those messages. Not only its appearance but also the way the building is utilized tell a great deal. Time and time again, it has been observed that when there is a relatively large investment in a building, the tendency is to protect that investment, to manicure it, to fence it in, to admire it from a distance. Imagine purchasing such expensive tools for the yard that they are cleaned, polished, oiled, and displayed for awed visitors but never used! Obviously, the weeds would take over very soon. Most people would not allow that to happen. However, the church building is a tool which, for pervasive but unknown reasons, tempts many toward being overprotective. When so tempted, consider that a slightly smudged, well-used church building is a much more beautiful symbol of God's power and involvement with humanity than a shiny, hands-off monument.

Closely related to maximum utilization is full accessibility. Certain popular architectural styles require spaces to be arranged so that there are awkward circulation patterns and steps which ignore the need of the handicapped and ill. On the other hand, if a building is designed from the inside out with meeting the needs of people as priority number one, no group will be eliminated because of the physical problem. A building that is accessible to all is beautiful.

Members who recently occupied the Mankato, Minnesota, Multi-Church Center received this letter: "The members of the Rotary Club wish to extend their most sincere appreciation for the use of the church building for the annual Christmas party for crippled children. This new building which is free of architectural barriers is an indication of the Christian concern that the members of the congregation have for those who are less able to manage steps. It is a very disheartening experience for the handicapped individual to have to be carried up and down stairs like freight. The new church building makes it possible for everyone to come together on a more equal basis." One does not even need to see a picture of this particular building to know that it is beautiful! This is consistent with the teachings of Christ, who excluded no one.

Beauty also contains a social element. Extravagance amidst human poverty or which contributes to that poverty is not beautiful. Extravagance should be defined in a broad way to include not only unnecessary frills but also those unwise choices which decrease the church's resources available for meeting human need. When, for the sake of convenience, a congregation rejects options, such as multiple sessions, shared facilities, or flexible space, tacit approval is given to spending more than is necessary on itself. The poor, the hungry, the homeless, the lonely, and the victims of injustice understand all too clearly the implications of such decisions. Again, the result is something less than simplicity or dynamic humility. "In the hands of a competent architect, [inexpensive buildings] can be buildings of equal beauty. The challenge of limited resources may enhance the beauty."[2]

[2]James F. White, "Church Architecture of the 1970s," *Liturgy* (May, 1975) p. 152. Reprinted with permission of the Liturgical Conference, 1221 Massachusetts Ave., NW, Washington, DC 20005.

A congregation may begin to move toward the achievement of this goal when it realizes that the most powerful visible symbol it has is the church building. In actual practice, church buildings become a part of the message their occupants are attempting to convey. Ministers may preach an hour or two each week, but the building proclaims its message twenty-four hours every day. The question thus arises, are the beliefs of the congregation affirmed by its physical plant or is there confusion or even contradiction? There are definitely some problems at this point. "Throughout America, towering pseudo-Gothic edifices house a faith that lies at the opposite pole of belief and practice from that of the Roman Catholic Church that inspired this style." [3] The same could be said for several other styles of church architecture. Such inconsistencies are much less likely to occur when design grows out of the beliefs of the members themselves.

Another guideline for consideration is that beauty incorporates a building design which appeals to the present and the future more than to the past. While rooted in events which occurred thousands of years ago, Christianity is nothing but stale history unless it provides meaning for today and hope for tomorrow. Symbols such as the cross, the table, the cup, and bread are reminders of Christ and form the basis for personal faith. The church building itself does not need to remind us of times gone by, particularly romanticized eras of two hundred or three hundred years ago.

In a large midwestern town there is a church building of traditional colonial architecture which stands in the middle of a section of several contemporary high-rise offices and apartments. This stately structure of red brick, white columns, tall windows, and crystal chandeliers literally shouts out, "Three cheers for the eighteenth century!" It might be asked, what was so outstanding about colonial America? Selective memories may filter out the negatives and remember only the quiet, idyllic rural life. It was, in fact, an age with joys and problems like any other. Many hardships were endured; slaves were bought and sold; colonists who came to America for religious freedom promptly denied it to others. Thus, the colonial style does not symbolize a perfect or even necessarily pure period of history.

Honest questions need to be faced as the church considers

[3] Albert Christ-Janer and Mary Mix Foley, *Modern Church Architecture* (New York: McGraw-Hill Book Company, Inc., 1962), p. 239. Used with permission.

construction. To which generations will the building primarily speak its message and serve? Will the design itself encourage clinging to an idealized past or reaching toward God's future of hope? Does the design offer comfort and challenge or escape from reality?

True beauty is not dependent upon any architectural style, whether it be colonial, Gothic, or contemporary. A building is beautiful when it is consistent with the message that its occupants are attempting to convey. The message of the church is not aimed exclusively at its own members. The message is for people who hurt, both within and outside the church, as well as a secular world which believes humankind can resolve its own problems without interference from God. So, it is important to consider what would appeal most to those not now a part of the institutional church. It is likely that such people are more concerned with today and tomorrow than with a history in which they had no part.

The response to this view may be that, in this rapidly changing era, what people most want is something eternal, secure, and permanent to help them maintain equilibrium within a churning world. While affirming that security is a universal need, we must also acknowledge that eternal truth requires constant, updated application. The dimension of eternity runs both ways, back to the beginning and forward to the consummation. People continually need an interpreter for the eternal at whatever point on the continuum they find themselves. If a teenager has difficulty understanding the King James Version of the Bible when reading it for the first time, imagine the additional agony should that initial encounter be with a Greek or Hebrew manuscript! Old Testament laws need reinterpretation for contemporary times. The challenge for church buildings is to symbolize the eternal without being self-contradictory by limiting that symbol to one particular age. To be successful in this quest is to find beauty. If such is impossible, the lesser sin is to elevate the present with all its ambiguities rather than to give an incomplete picture of some idealized past day.

Another guideline to consider is that beauty includes conserving natural resources and energy. The desperate need for such conservation was discussed in the previous chapter. The point here is that any aesthetic judgment must now include criteria relating to the use of natural resources. A beautiful building will be one which does its job effectively while extracting the least possible amount of materials from the earth for its erection, use, and maintenance.

Careful thought should be given both to the materials of construction and to the systems which heat, cool, and light the building.

One criteria is whether the material is replaceable or recyclable. Lumber, for example, is replaceable under a planned program of reforestation. Scrap steel may be recycled. Unless restricted by building codes, materials that do not meet these tests should be avoided. Most present fuels are irreplaceable. Thus, heavy insulation to minimize the use of fuel, orientation of the building to take advantage of the winter sun, and the use of solar power are all options deserving consideration.

The energy cost of materials is another criteria. Aluminum, for example, requires relatively large amounts of inefficiently generated electricity for its manufacture. Whenever possible, utilize materials that need the lowest level of energy consumption for their production and transportation to the construction site.

Although the use of solar or wind energy has been the subject of widespread conversation for only a brief period of time, people are already objecting to the appearance of solar panels or windmills either on or near a building. Sometimes this equipment can be incorporated into the design so as to be hardly noticeable. More often, however, such integral design is impossible for a variety of reasons (especially when retrofitting an existing structure) or so expensive as to be impractical. What then? Should the church reject the long-term saving of natural resources (and, incidentally, money) on the grounds that the building "wouldn't look right" with some solar panels on the roof?

One philosophy of contemporary church design contends that it is more honest and natural to expose basic construction materials than to cover them. The flying buttress of a medieval Gothic church building was exposed by necessity because the engineering was not available to hide this essential, supporting structure. While the techniques are now at hand to disguise such elements as laminated wood beams, roof decking, and the marks of poured concrete forms, architects often choose not to hide them for both artistic and economic reasons. Such materials have a strength and attractiveness of their own, so why take the time and expense to cover them up?

While creative design will integrate all elements in as pleasing a way as possible, there should not be too much anxiety about the appearance of building materials that conserve natural resources. They announce to the community that the church takes seriously its own teachings about stewardship and is deeply concerned for the survival and abundant life of future generations. Perhaps the church of tomorrow will openly profess its stance by having a building with several, large south-facing windows, solar collectors and solar cells on the roof, and a windmill churning out electricity right where the steeple might have been. The beauty of such a building would be far more than skin deep. It would say as much or more to the needs of the people of its day as did any Gothic cathedral or columned, colonial edifice.

A final guideline for consideration is that beauty means being consistent with the setting. Church buildings constructed on a monumental scale tend to dominate their surroundings. Illustrating the power and majesty of God may have been the original motivation, but the result has often been interpreted as an untouchable majesty, a power too remote from daily human need to be of much use. In a residential area. a church building more on a domestic scale may symbolize the attitude of acceptance and caring. "We are more inclined now to look at a church [building] as a social part of the townscape which fits in with its neighbors rather than as a monument which dominates them."[4]

The implication is not intended that the church should melt into its surroundings, acceding to the imperfections of the community. The message of the church is prophetic, judging all against the standard of Christ, and whatever facility is used should symbolize this message in some way. However, even as the Lord met people where they were and challenged them with what they could become, so the church needs a starting point for communication. If that starting point, as symbolized by the church building, is too far removed from the experiential situation of the potential constituent, dialogue will not even begin.

Perhaps this is a reason why storefront churches are often successful in declining, low-income neighborhoods. They meet the constituent at her or his point of need, standing within the cluster of small shops that regularly meet other needs of the urban poor. Sometimes the only symbol used is a small cross in the window. This viewpoint should be studied more thoroughly as the church attempts to minister to people, such as office workers in skyscrapers, apartment dwellers, and weekend campers/recreational enthusiasts.

[4] White, *op. cit.*

A long-distance traveler may suffer "jet lag" in trying to catch up with the time at the point of destination. The church cannot afford to impose, by the design of its facility, a "cultural lag" upon those who are the objects of its message. A beautiful building is one which fits in naturally with the daily environment of those toward whom ministry is directed.

One cannot read the preceding guidelines, take pencil to paper, and immediately design a beautiful church building. Instead, these are subjects for the congregation to ponder and share with their architect long before the time for design. It is hoped that this might be a starting point for thought and discussion about what is truly beautiful in the design of church buildings.

What Can the Church Afford? 7

In planning for building or remodeling, the amount a church can afford is obviously important. In this context, economy means the best, most serviceable space for the dollar. This is quite different from the largest amount of space per dollar spent. Not the quantity but the usability is most important. Areas that are adaptable will cost somewhat more initially than single-use rooms because of the material and equipment needed for flexibility, such as movable partitions and furnishings, carpet and other items required for acoustical control. However, flexible areas are far more economical overall because less total space is needed and rooms may be utilized more often. As described previously, the *usage cost* per square foot is lower, as well as maintenance and utilities expenditures, and these are the most important considerations for true economy.

Another gauge of economy is the cost per year of service. It is not only the initial price but also the quality of building materials that matters. Church buildings should be constructed of materials that are durable enough to last for a reasonable period of time. If poorly constructed, major repairs may be needed before the mortgage is retired. In the long run, a so-called "cheap" structure may turn out to be very expensive.

While reasonable quality is important, the other side of this issue is that poorly designed and inflexible church buildings which are too durably constructed may become more of a burden than a blessing. This is a day of change in which congregations vary relatively rapidly in their size and composition because of shifting neighborhood, employment, and economic patterns. But instead of a tent that can be folded and moved to meet new needs, the church may own a fortress-like, permanent edifice. It has been the experience of many a congregation that such a building inhibits ministry.

It is certainly possible for a community to be so stable that a church building can function effectively for many generations. In that case, the most durably built structure would be best for long-term economy. However, the number of such locations in America seems to be decreasing rapidly. Also, it is nearly impossible to forecast accurately what will happen to any community over sixty, forty, or even twenty years. There is no easy answer to this dilemma.

One option is to build with future conversion possibilities in mind. Unless the congregation happens to own a valuable piece of land, the used, traditional church building is difficult to market because of the specialized type of structure normally involved. To whom does one sell a typical church building? About the only buyer is another congregation with limited resources, so that the seller is not likely to receive fair market value. With that door virtually shut the congregation may be unable to remedy its situation. But suppose the building was so designed that conversion to offices or classrooms or recreation space or housing is relatively easy? Then the possibilities for sale increase along with the chances for receiving a fair price.

If this option sounds radical, it is because a radical solution is needed. Unknown millions of church resource dollars have been lost because no one asked the question, "What will we do with our building later on if changes require relocation or a major shift in the emphasis of our ministry?" If this question *is* asked, a capable architect can design attractive and functional church facilities which may be converted at a later date to usage for other purposes. In this event, the use of quality materials giving service for sixty to one hundred years without major expenditures would be a wise purchase for true, long-term economy.

Renovation or New Construction

One question about affordability relates to the cost of major renovations as compared to that of new construction. A congregation in Pennsylvania owns a building that is about seventy-five years old. It is a well-maintained, attractive structure in a community that prides itself on its historical homes and public buildings. But some rather expensive repairs are now needed. Before granting a building permit for such extensive work, the city could well require bringing the entire facility up to current building and fire codes, which will be costly. How can a church know whether to renovate or rebuild?

Both cost and program effectiveness help to determine the answer. The arrangement of a building may be such that a church cannot function the way it wishes today. The program decisions literally set in concrete decades ago cannot be altered without extremely expensive structural changes. For example, small cell-like classrooms with load-bearing walls make it impossible to have larger groupings for active student participation in learning experiences, discussion groups, or the open classroom, team-teaching concept. A sanctuary with a sloping floor prohibits many types of participative worship experiences. In such cases, although some renovation might be possible from a cost standpoint, the result would not help the church to minister in the relevant way that it may desire. Thus the question of program compatibility must be answered satisfactorily if recycling is to be feasible.

Should the space present no significant obstacles to effective programming, the question of financial practicality must then be resolved. When is the cost of recycling an older building too high? Objective, professional assistance is needed here. The inspection and written report of an engineering firm (structural and mechanical) will state clearly the condition of the building and its future requirements. Engineers who are not members of the church and who have no financial stake in the eventual decision would be best for this work. The cost of this service (it could be $1,000 or more) is well worth it, considering the hours of discussion about the condition of the building that otherwise usually occur among church members who do not have the thorough and detailed technical data necessary to make an informed judgment. Many members have often already formed opinions based mainly on feelings and emotional ties to the past. Instead, a feasibility study and cost analysis should be carefully prepared by engineers and/or architects covering such items as:

1. A thorough, on-site visual inspection of the church building, including structure, interior and exterior walls, ceilings, floors, roof, supporting beams and braces, windows, stairs, walks, plumbing, heating, air conditioning, electrical system, insulation, and energy efficiency.

2. Determination whether the building meets fire, safety, parking,

and building codes of the community, listing work that must be done to meet code requirements; estimation of the useful remaining life of the present building.

3. Review of the program goals adopted by the church; itemized estimate of the cost of renovations required to meet these goals.

4. Itemized estimate of the cost of repairs necessary for safety and to meet code requirements.

5. Replacement cost estimation for the building using projected prices of one year from the date of the report and space needs based upon the degree of flexibility allowed by the congregation. (If relocation is desirable, include estimated proceeds from sale of present property and estimated cost of new land.)

6. Comparison and analysis of remodeling versus rebuilding based upon both financial and program criteria.

7. Recommendation as to whether remodeling or rebuilding is more feasible.

This type of thorough analysis will probably take three to five working days, perhaps about equally divided between on-site research and writing of the report. Sometimes the engineer's report will clearly indicate that either remodeling or rebuilding is the obvious solution. At other times, the evidence may be about equal on both sides. When there appears to be a stalemate, the church could turn to the experiences of others. The author's contacts with such congregations have led to the conclusion that when a church must spend as much as 40 to 50 percent of the cost of an adequate new structure to remodel an old building or make it suitable for their needs, such renovation is probably not cost effective in the long term.

There are certainly several additional factors which will have high priority for some churches. One is the desire to remain compatible with a well-preserved, historic neighborhood. Another is the willingness to live with some program inadequacies or parking inconveniences in order to keep ministering to the same area. In some cases, a scarcity of energy or materials plus higher prices makes the recycling of older buildings more feasible. Depending upon the wishes of the church and the needs of the moment, such factors might be decisive. Otherwise, the "over 40 percent factor" mentioned in the previous paragraph could be a guide in reaching the delicate decision about whether to renovate or rebuild. (It should also be recognized that cost estimates for both renovation and new construction have a tendency to be less than actual bids for the work.)

Timing

A second important area relates to the timing for a building or renovation project. *When* can a church afford to take action? The vast majority of congregations are unprepared to face large capital expenditures at the time the need arises. The reasons for this are puzzling. The church sometimes forgets its own theology which teaches that all physical things will decay. A newspaper story once stated that a woman "died unexpectedly at age 95." In the same vein, many congregations face "unexpected" building repairs or replacement at age ninety-five or far younger.

The logical procedure to avoid large, traumatic expenses over a few years is to budget a small amount *every* year designated specifically and exclusively for major capital needs. When its mortgages are all paid off, the church that so designates 3 to 5 percent of every annual budget will normally have enough from the principal and interest on the savings to remodel or build when the need arises. Since most churches do not follow this procedure, however, the subject of timing tends to become a divisive issue.

On the one hand are those staunch backers of the cash concept who want to wait until every dollar is in before any work begins. While this may be an admirable theory, unless some plan of saving has been followed over many years, as was advocated in the previous paragraph, waiting for cash on hand is no longer realistic. Because of the time normally required to accumulate funds for a special purpose from the regular budget, it is difficult to maintain a high level of enthusiasm and giving. During those years, inflation devaluates the dollars collected. (No one is predicting an end to inflation, and costs in the construction field are rising faster than those in the general economy.) Therefore, most churches that try this procedure over the short term find that, five or ten years later, they have actually lost ground.

On the other hand, there are those anxious to move forward immediately by borrowing all they can for as long as they can or by accepting facilities of poor quality or both. The negative consequences of this procedure for future decades are obvious. Even though the need may be quite urgent, there are still some basic guidelines that should be followed to achieve a satisfactory experience.

For one thing, the facility improvement should be made in time to prevent a declining ministry, if at all possible. Because of rapidly changing circumstances, some churches cannot afford to postpone needed work. Any church must attract new members if it is to live. While loyal, long-time members may be able to tolerate almost any kind of building problem, those who might otherwise be attracted to the church judge from a different perspective. Major capital expenditures may thus be a necessity for the congregation to survive. While the improvements may not be possible immediately, a vigorous plan of action aimed toward a realistic goal two or three years away will demonstrate to potential members the intent of the church.

Another guideline is that at least 25 percent of the total funds necessary should be accumulated by the time construction work is finished. This gives a goal to work toward and helps in estimating a realistic time schedule. With these assets on hand, the loan amount required should be within the ability of the congregation to repay over a reasonable period of time.

Experience indicates that it is best if the loan for church facility improvements has an amortization period of fifteen years or less. The "down payment" of at least 25 percent and the scope of the building project should be arranged so that monthly payments allow the loan to be retired in no more that fifteen years. The reason for this is two-fold. First, a longer amortization period results in excessive payments of interest. For example, on a loan of $100,000 at $8\frac{1}{2}\%$, $77,253 in interest is required over a fifteen-year amortization period. For thirty years, the same loan requires $176,811 in interest, an additional amount of interest nearly equal to the original $100,000 loan!

The other main reason for a shorter loan amortization period is that most churches want to do some rearranging, redecorating, remodeling, or other facility improvement work every twelve to fifteen years. If mortgage payments are still required for an additional five, ten, or fifteen years at the time, either such needed improvements are not done or the congregation falls behind in making loan payments.

Still another subject related to timing is the schedule to be followed by the architect. While preliminary plans are necessary to allow members to picture the facility improvement as a motivation for their giving, *no further work* should be done by the architect until the church is assured of financing sufficient to meet its projected budget. This is a most important point which, if followed, can spare the congregation much grief over aborted plans as well as save money.

A large church in a university town decided to relocate. The architect was instructed to complete all the working drawings and specifications and then put the project out for construction bids before financing had been secured. When the bids came in very high, the church was forced to redesign on a smaller scale because the larger loan necessary was beyond their ability to repay. Over $10,000 worth of detailed plans and specifications were discarded. Months of time were lost and many members felt short-changed. Such disappointments can be avoided if logical procedures for the timing of events in proper sequence are followed.

These are the types of issues which need to be considered as a church contemplates the best time schedule for those major capital expenditures necessary in any construction project.

Cost of Debt Retirement

Another important question for consideration is how much the church can afford to pay each month for building debt retirement. What percentage of the budget should go for this purpose? This is a subject of balance, of proportion, and of priorities. The church building is only a tool for ministry. It ought to be a servant, not the master. At what percentage point in the church's budget do building needs take over and dictate the program for a number of years?

Even as individual consumers must be careful that their debt ratio remains within a solvent, realistic range, so must the church be vigilant at this point. Furthermore, the church is responsible for witnessing to the world that it is performing a vital ministry to people instead of spending too much on "overhead" mainly to serve itself.

Church expenditures often fall into four general categories: missions or benevolences, program, operations, and staff. A church that gives 25 percent or more to missions is relatively rare even though that kind of high percentage is usually an obvious indication of concern for others. Staff expenses represent a ministry to both members and nonmembers, but usually more to members. In a small church, staff costs may account for 50 percent or more of the annual budget. Program includes the important ministries to members and the community which often receive too few budget dollars. Operations includes everything necessary to enable the congregation to serve effectively, including buildings, utilities, and maintenance. For the most part, operations is a support function and, therefore, the less money required to do an adequate job, the better.

When there is no yearly investment in a capital improvement

savings fund and when careful long-range planning is neglected, a church can find itself faced with the unattractive prospect of committing over 50 percent of its annual income to debt retirement for ten, twelve, or more years. By any measure, this is a situation of imbalance which hinders the true ministry of the congregation. Some time ago a church in Ohio was overoptimistic in its projections and built a large building of single-use, inflexible space years ahead of the time when the peak attendance was supposed to be reached. A twenty-year loan was secured. At the ten-year point, anticipated growth had not come and much space stood empty and unused. But the mortgage payments had to be made for ten more years, requiring over 50 percent of annual income. The overworked pastor was most frustrated because there was no money for new programs or help of any kind, even secretarial.

The preceding example illustrates what can happen when there is insufficient planning, the wrong kind of space is constructed, and too much is borrowed for too long a period of time. When these things occur, almost all of the energy of the church over a ten- to twenty-year period is focused on constructing and paying for its building. The thoughtful congregation deeply concerned about its witness and ministry to people will attempt to avoid this kind of imbalance in its priorities.

Experience indicates that the "safe" range of expenditure for building debt retirement is between 20 and 35 percent of the total annual church budget. A recent study of one denomination indicated that 82 percent of their church construction loans approved required less than 35 percent of the annual budget for mortgage payments. If the mortgage retirement rate exceeds 35 percent of the annual budget, there are either some rather unusual circumstances or, as is almost always the case, giving to missions is very low and church programs of ministry to people suffer from lack of funds during the duration of the mortgage. Every congregation contemplating facility improvements will want to examine carefully all the consequences of this crucial decision.

The Construction Budget

To determine what the church can afford without jeopardizing its ongoing ministry, the renovation or construction budget should be prepared accurately quite early in the process and include all possible elements. The first discussion about costs is usually very unrealistic.

Expectations can be raised to a level that is difficult to adjust later. Members picture a certain budgetary amount without realizing the necessary expenses which must be considered. Often the situation is compounded by an overly optimistic, low estimate of the cost of construction. Because of an inherent conflict of interest, the architect will seldom ask detailed questions about the construction budget established by the church. To avoid later disappointment, the congregation must therefore know what it can really afford.

At the time when an architect is selected, the construction budget should be included in the architect-owner contract or else accompany it in clear, written form. The figure given is the *net* amount, that is, the dollars allocated to the construction project exclusive of all other necessary costs. Here is the point where confusion often arises. It is common for 20 percent, 25 percent, or more of the total project cost to go for needed items other than construction itself. There is a degree of similarity here with the cost of an automobile. The base price of a car does not include such costs as sales tax, transportation, license, preparation charges, and/or import duties. These necessities add considerably to the actual purchase price. (In the budget which will now be described and which is contained in Appendix E, these items relating to church buildings are covered in detail.)

Resources

The construction budget begins with the listing of available resources. This includes all funds currently on hand which may be utilized for the project, including savings certificates, stocks, bonds, and cash. Next comes a projection of income from the current date until the estimated construction completion date. (The architect or planning consultant can advise as to the possible time for construction.) The average monthly building fund income for the past six to twelve months may be used for this projection. If a special Capital Funds Campaign (CFC) is scheduled, the income should increase considerably after that campaign, and this change needs to be taken into account.

How much can a church raise in a special Capital Funds Campaign? Obviously, this depends upon such factors as motivation, unity, timing, congregational income, and economic conditions. In a 2½ year study covering 1974–1976, one denomination found an average pledge per giving (or family) unit of $775 for three years. Over $6,000,000 was raised in these efforts led by a skilled, professional director. Care must be exercised in using such statistics as anything more than "ballpark estimates," especially if there is no experienced campaign director involved.

Another resource is the borrowing potential of the church. This subject was covered in the preceding section in regard to the proportion of the total budget which allows a balanced ministry. A yearly loan repayment schedule not exceeding 35 percent of the total budget is recommended. Another guideline relates to the projected level of pledging in the major financial effort. A typical CFC covers a three-year period. Experience indicates that a loan amount (15-year amortization) equal to approximately 2 times the total pledges from a three-year campaign is normally feasible. If the campaign duration is different than three years or if no CFC is held, another way of stating this is that, for a fifteen-year loan, an indebtedness six times the annual building fund income would be considered possible for many churches, without major disruptions to their programs of ministry.

It is obvious that the determination of borrowing potential is not an easy task for any church, nor is there a precise means of measurement. It is also clear that unusual circumstances may justify exceptions to general guidelines such as these. However, because the loan usually becomes such a large part of the total building budget, it is best to be on the conservative side in making early estimates. It is far better to find later that there is some extra money available than to come up short and be forced to retreat from built-up hopes.

One other resource that may apply in certain circumstances is the sale of property. In case of relocation, this could be the present church building and land. It could also be the parsonage or adjacent land that is not needed or property that was given as a gift to the congregation. For purposes of the preliminary construction budget, such property should be valued realistically.

There are many "values" that can be applied to a building of any type. There is a *sentimental value* which depends upon the kinds of important experiences that can be associated with the structure. Events such as marriage, the raising of children, family reunions, business success, or deep spiritual experiences can be related to the home, park, office, or church where they took place. The experience certainly did not depend upon the environment in which it occurred, but memory relates the two, and thus there are sentimental values as varied and different as is humanity.

Another value is a *utilitarian value,* related to usage. A building which was basically designed for one purpose, such as a bowling alley, may be very valuable if bowling facilities are needed. But if the need at a later date is for an indoor tennis court, for example, the expensive, specialized space and equipment of the bowling alley may be of little value. It is of no use to describe the quality of the pins, the perfect balance of the balls, or the beautifully waxed hardwood alleys if the need is for tennis courts. Unless a building is flexible enough to be converted to meet different requirements, its value will be determined by the demand for that particular kind of structure.

Still another value has to do with timing, the *current value.* A building designed to house a blacksmith shop, or one to freeze and encapsulate scientists for a lengthy journey to outer space, would be of little value right now since the time for their usage is either past or future.

One other value is that of *location.* A service station located one block from the main highway will be worth a fraction of the value of a station that is on the highway itself. The location of a building relative to its constituents, accessible roads, and parking can greatly affect its worth.

All of these factors have an influence on the real value of a church building. It is important to realize that the sentimental value may influence the thinking of members, but it will not influence others. They will be thinking instead of the utilitarian, location, and current values.

Begin with an appraisal by a professional realtor who is approved as a Master Appraiser (MAI) by the Institute of Real Estate Appraisers and who is not a member of the church. Even experienced realtors find it difficult to give an accurate estimate of the value of their own church building because the sentimental value affects their thinking. Such a realtor once told the building committee of his church that was relocating to accept no less than $80,000 for the old property. Months later, after considerable effort, the sale netted $18,000. As has been stated previously, traditional church buildings of inflexible design have very limited possibilities for sale unless the land is strategically located and, thus, of high value.

Even with a professional appraisal, the worth of any property is not fully determined until there is an interested, qualified buyer with a signed contract in hand. Thus, even the appraisal figure should be reduced when first drawing up the budget. The percentage of reduction depends upon the best estimates as to when the property will be sold. If a potential purchaser has already shown interest by signing an option to buy (usually for 90 or 120 days), a reduction of 10 to 20 percent in the appraised figure would be appropriate to cover expenses of selling and a possible eventual decrease in the price. On the other hand, if chances for sale within a year or two appear dim, probably nothing should be included for this item on the resource side of the budget.

Several years ago, a church in a small industrial town decided to relocate. The full appraised value of their property was included in the budget, and their architects designed accordingly. A large manufacturing plant had closed there sometime before, so prospects for the local economy were not great. Months turned into years, and the old church property failed to sell. Finally, the new building plans were abandoned at a cost of thousands of dollars and a different course of action was taken. If the original plans had been designed according to a more realistic budget, a smaller, phased building could have been projected, and an early move might have allowed an expanded ministry. Then, whenever the old building sold, an addition could have been built in the new location. This experience illustrates the need to review sales prospects carefully before adding any contemplated proceeds to the projected budget.

Related Expenses

The next section of the construction budget includes those related expenses normally necessary to complete a project. This money does not buy bricks or lumber but rather necessary services and items that are not an integrated, attached part of the building. Usually these costs are proportional to the extent and complexity of the project. (Some of the items that follow may not need to be included if the church has decided upon remodeling rather than new construction.)

In estimating expenses for the purpose of preparing a realistic budget, some elements will be more difficult to determine because they are expressed in terms of a percentage of the construction cost. Since that amount is not known until after all the resources and expenses are included, a "guesstimate" must first be made and then adjusted up or down depending upon the result of the calculations. For example, if the architect's fee is 9 percent and a review of both resources and expenses indicates that the net construction budget will be in the vicinity of $300,000, a figure of $27,000 is inserted for the architect's fee. Other costs expressed by percentages will also be inserted, based upon the $300,000 estimate. Then, after the calculations are made, the estimate is adjusted up or down depending upon whether the net construction budget totals above or below $300,000. Two or three such adjustments by a person who is mathematically inclined will usually result in a list of projected expenses that is quite accurate.

The category of professional expenses includes fees for the architect (which covers engineering), planning and financial consultants (if used), and an attorney. The architect may work for a flat fee or a percentage of the construction costs. If there is a stated dollar amount, the church should request a contract based on an hourly rate with the total "not to exceed" a specified sum. There is a potential savings in this if the work takes fewer hours than the architect had anticipated. If more time is required, the church still does not pay more than the stated amount. Should the architect work on a percentage basis, the fee could range from 6 to 12 percent or more, depending upon the scope of the project. Remodeling, for example, requires higher fees. Generally, the larger and less complicated the project, the lower the percentage fee.

An attorney is needed to review all legal documents, such as contracts, mortgages, notes, and deeds. Usually attorneys work on an hourly basis and will give estimates on their costs for the church. A church planning and building consultant may be available without cost from the parent denomination or may require a percentage or flat fee. Many congregations can testify to the value of using experienced, professional consultants. One or two small suggestions can save far more than the modest fee involved. The same can be said for a financial consultant or Capital Funds Campaign Director. Several denominations provide this service and it is also available from commercial organizations. Fees are usually based upon the length of the campaign and the membership of the church.

Furnishings and equipment that are not built into the structure form another expense category. This may involve such items as tables, chairs, desks, movable storage cabinets, pianos, files, typewriters, office machines, and addressing equipment. If the worship area is included, the cost multiplies because of the nature and large quantity of furnishings usually required. Such items as chairs or pews and chancel furnishings are expensive. Because of its high price, the organ, if needed, is listed separately. A pipe organ will be from two to six times as expensive, initially, as a good electronic organ. (The projected lifetime costs of organs should be thoroughly reviewed and compared before purchase.)

In some situations, the church may need to pay for new property or the demolition of an old building. If demolition is necessary, materials in the existing facility may be of enough value that there will be no charge for removal, or payment may even be received for the used building materials. This needs to be checked out with demolition companies, however, because in most cases there is a charge for such work.

Another category is miscellaneous expenses which include the topographical survey, soil testing, landscaping, insurance, and interest during construction. The survey and soil testing are needed for new construction and are not included in the architect's fee. The survey indicates property elevations, contours, utility and tree locations, building setback requirements, and any existing easements. This is required by the architect prior to serious preliminary design work. If a new site is being considered, soil testing may be advisable prior to purchase or be included as a contingency of the sale, especially if there is any previous record or suspicion of soil problems. Soil testing reveals the type and density of earth materials beneath the surface. It has implications for the location, footings, and structure of the building. Estimates for both the survey and soil testing may be obtained from surveyors and soil engineers.

Whether remodeling or building anew, the church is responsible for a portion of the insurance during construction apart from the insurance liability carried by contractors. This involves completed parts of the building and materials on the site that have been paid for. Included are items such as theft, vandalism, and storm damage. This responsibility is best explained by the church's own insurance agent. The cost is minimal but should still be included in the budget.

If borrowing funds, the church will be paying interest each month during the construction period on the amount of money that has been used to date. Full payments of both principal and interest usually do not begin until after construction is completed. The amount for interest during construction needs to be estimated, for it usually comes to several thousand dollars. This may be figured by multiplying one-half the amount being borrowed by the annual interest rate, then multiply this total by the portion of a year over which the loan money is used. This will be the approximate amount of interest that needs to be included in the budget.

For example, suppose that $200,000 is being borrowed at 8½% annual interest. The construction is to take ten months, but funds already in hand cover the first three months of contractor's bills. The budgeted amount for interest during construction should then be:

$$\frac{\$200,000}{2} \times 8\tfrac{1}{2}\% \times 7/12 = \$4,958.33$$

In new construction, if planting the lawn and providing trees, bushes, and other landscaping are not included in the contractor's bid, an estimated amount should be a part of budget expenses. One other category which it is very wise to include is that of contingencies. This is for items that, according to Webster, are "possible, but not certain, to occur." One quite certain possibility is inflation. Check with people such as contractors and bankers in the area to learn what the inflation rate has been in the construction industry over the past year. Apply this rate to the time remaining until bids are received. For the budget, this estimate is developed in the same manner as with the architect's percentage fee previously described. Because of the unforeseen delays which so often occur, using a time period of at least one year is usually recommended. If accurate current statistics are not available, use an annual inflation rate of approximately 10 percent. (There is a "Comparative Cost Multiplier" guide available which gives the inflation factor each quarter for various types of buildings in western, central, and eastern geographical areas. This may be obtained from Marshall & Swift Publishing Co., Los Angeles.)

Another contingency expense to consider is needed items that were inadvertently omitted from the construction bidding documents. Even when it seems that everything is carefully scrutinized throughout the entire project, something inevitably comes up at the last minute. Thankfully, it is normally a small item that was missed, but it is usually important enough that problems can arise if the funds are not available. Therefore, it would be most helpful if a small budget figure, such as 2 percent, could be included.

The final step in formulating a realistic estimated construction budget is to subtract total related expenses from the projected total resources. This gives the *net* budget which is the actual figure available for construction work and which the architect should use for design purposes. As was stated at the beginning of this section, the net budget could well be at least 20 percent less than the total resources available. It is extremely important for the congregation to know this at the earliest possible stage of planning. When all the costs are figured, the church will have a better idea of what it can afford.

Y

Raising and Borrowing Funds 8

If the church decides that major renovations or a new building or some other type of construction work is advisable, a special financial campaign is usually required. A regular, long-term savings plan involving a small percentage of the annual church budget (as previously advocated) would reduce or eliminate this need. Unless such a plan has been used, however, an intensive effort is often essential to raise sufficient funds within a time span short enough to help offset the eroding effects of inflation.

Fund Raising Methods

The experience of many churches is that a financial campaign for facility improvements is most successful when conducted separately from the annual, general budget appeal. The strength of "unified giving" is that there can be a balance among many legitimate needs without exhausting the giver by appealing for each one separately. The weakness of this philosophy is that it does not recognize the fact that people give most to those causes which are of highest personal priority to them. When the entire church has affirmed the top priority of a construction project, the appeal is usually made for designated pledges to that project without reducing giving to the general budget.

The timing for a major financial campaign is directly related to its chances for success. A premature appeal will result in cautious, minimal response. Sometimes, before any decisions have been made, a church will decide to "test the wind" by asking members what they might give if some kind of a building project is held in the future. It would certainly be a mistake to take response from such an appeal seriously. This could, in fact, serve to halt the research necessary to determine whether facility improvements are needed and, if so, what they should be. People need to be active participants in the decision making and have some visual idea of what the project will include if they are going to make a maximum commitment.

If the congregational planning discussed in chapter 1 results in a decision to enter some type of construction project, the next step is to employ an architect. With both program goals and budget limitations firmly in mind, the architect prepares preliminary (schematic) designs. These include floor plans and elevations for review and eventual approval by the congregation. When members affirm the way their decisions have taken three-dimensional shape (as illustrated by a perspective drawing, floor plans, and/or a model), they are then at the point of highest motivation for giving. A financial campaign held soon after approval of the preliminary design usually has the best chance for success.

While less important than the subject just considered, the time of the year when a financial effort occurs is also a factor. It is best to avoid the usual time of extreme weather for the area, popular vacation weeks, Easter, Thanksgiving, and Christmas. If there is congregational unity and the motivation is high, however, successful financial campaigns have been held every week of the year. When the subject of timing is resolved, the key question is, *how* shall the church raise the needed funds?

Sales and Raffles

One fairly popular method is to conduct rummage and other types of sales, raffles, lotteries, and the like. While used often, it is best to review thoroughly both the motivations and the results of such procedures. A midwestern church decided not to use the professional financial consultants of their denomination to help raise funds for a much-needed building project. Instead, they conducted a "low-key" pledging effort on their own and supplemented its poor results with parking lot sales and raffles. In the meantime, inflation continued and, five years later, they were little closer to their goal than in the beginning.

Procedures of this type could be considered as amateur business operations. When goods or lottery tickets are sold to nonmembers, the church has completed a business transaction and placed the profit in the building fund. When a member buys, the motivation is a mixture of charity and wanting to receive something of value in return. If a member produces some handwork for sale, more faithfulness is shown, but, unless that person has no income from which to give, total commitment may still be missing. All such procedures need to be compared with the biblical concept of stewardship.

Sales and raffles may have a place in providing supplemental income for furnishings or equipment, but most churches that count on this source for major capital funds are disappointed. The same result may be expected if community businesses are approached for donations. There are so many churches and synagogues that most businesses refuse or make only a token gift in order to avoid the charge of discrimination. The church should look to its own constituency to support needed facility improvement projects.

Selling of bonds

Another relatively widespread method of financing is the selling of bonds. Governmental units often sell bonds to finance needed projects. In the church, however, members need to be clear about the difference between investing and giving. To invest is to expect fair payment (interest) for use of the money and the return of the principal when the investment matures. The Christian concept of stewardship involves giving out of love with no thought of return.

When people understand the distinction between investing and giving, they will realize that buying bonds means making a loan to the church. But selling bonds does not indicate anything about how that loan is to be repaid. A financial effort which receives offerings from members is still needed to give a solid basis for repayment. The problem is that bond purchasers feel they have already given and do not always respond to a financial campaign. Many bond-selling campaigns include the assumption or hope, however, that the person who buys bonds is really giving, not investing. At the very least, this is misrepresentation, a deception that does not meet the standards of Christian ethics. Years later, there is often an expensive surprise when the bondholders actually want their money back. If used at all, bond sales should be clearly labeled as investments and take place only after a financial effort has confirmed the ability of the church to repay.

In order to be effective, bond sales must equal or exceed the amount needed for the project. The church needs to be prepared for the possibility that total sales may not reach the amount required to finance construction. If this occurs, sales are often extended to nonmembers. In these cases, the church needs to recognize that such nonmembers are definitely investing, not contributing. If total sales never reach the required amount, either the scope of the project must be reduced or all bonds are returned and other means of financing are sought. In this case, the money paid to have the bond program is forfeited.

A bond program requires a very disciplined procedure for repayment. Bonds are usually sold for specific periods of maturity, such as five, ten, fifteen, and twenty years in contrast to standard mortgage loan repayments which are the same, level amount every month. If there is a five-year period between payments, it is very tempting for the church to use incoming building fund offerings for other urgent needs rather than setting the money aside to make bond payments. Thus, too often churches have found themselves faced with a large bond payment without the necessary funds available.

There are two other potential problems closely related to this subject of timing. One is that the sale of too many bonds in the shorter maturity series can result in the need to refinance before all of the bonds are repaid. Unlike mortgage loans, bonds can and usually have an uneven curve of cash-flow required for debt service. The other possibility is that payments increase toward the end of the program because higher interest is paid for the longer maturity bonds. To overcome the problems inherent in the uneven payment schedule of a bond program, the church must be able to project its income very accurately and be adamant in its resolve not to touch those funds for any other purpose, however worthy.

Another area of concern is the question of how to treat objectively and fairly church members who are also lenders. A financial institution such as a bank is basically a permanent organization and is somewhat impersonal in its dealings, which is often an advantage where finances are involved. In contrast, church members at times face unexpected transfers or financial reverses which require cashing their bonds ahead of schedule. If the church is not in a position to repay early, disunity and hurt feelings may occur.

Over the course of fifteen or twenty years, it is not uncommon for a church to have a period of low activity, attendance, and income for many reasons, such as neighborhood decline, community economic woes, natural disaster, or pastoral or lay leadership problems. Should such a problem occur, the mortgage holder is usually willing to negotiate a revised payment schedule. No financial institution wants to foreclose on a church. This is quite different, however, from telling bondholders that the funds are not on hand to pay them, especially if whatever problem the church is having affects them personally.

Finally, the expense of conducting a bond sales program usually exceeds the cost involved in securing a mortgage loan. If the church is unable to receive a loan from its denomination or a community financial institution, it needs to consider carefully whether the contemplated project is financially sound. The possibility of selling bonds should be thoroughly investigated and compared with other loan sources before it is adopted. While the motivation of lending to one's own congregation at an expected interest savings may be commended by some, the potential problems need to be recognized and evaluated carefully.

Capital Funds Campaign

The method of raising funds for capital improvement projects which is most common and probably most valid for the church is the seeking of pledges "over and above" regular tithes and offerings through a special Capital Funds Campaign. While church members often say that they do not believe in pledging, there are several reasons why pledging is a valid approach. When people marry or enter into any kind of legal agreement or purchase anything on credit or sign a mortgage, they are pledging their word and their money that they will follow through on their promises. Making a commitment to a building fund for several years follows the same principle. Pledging is an act of faith in partnership with God.

Pledging also has the very practical result of indicating a level of church income sufficient to meet mortgage payments. This is normally required by financial institutions as a prerequisite for approval of a loan. Without the regular giving that pledging fosters, it is more difficult to obtain a loan. A financial institution usually likes to observe at least six months of giving following pledging as evidence that the commitments made are being honored.

Several national church bodies have professional CFC directors. Some former pastors work individually in this field, and there are several commercial companies which provide fund-raising counsel for nonprofit organizations. Experience has determined that, under normal circumstances, it is best to seek pledges for three years. A shorter period of time does not provide the stability needed to affirm the long-term intentions of the congregation. On the other hand, people are quite mobile today and changes occur so rapidly that, even with strong faith, they find it difficult to make a commitment for much longer than three years. At the end of the pledging period, an additional Capital Funds Campaign may be needed unless the church membership and giving have increased sufficiently so that the mortgage payment can be incorporated into the annual budget.

A CFC is an intensive effort of from one to eight weeks, depending upon the size of the membership. It involves much publicity regarding the proposed project. A specific dollar goal is usually established by congregational leaders with guidance from the campaign director. Since the best results come from person-to-person visits in the homes of constituents, a thorough training period for callers is required. As the time approaches for pledging, a large all-church meeting or dinner is often held to explain the purpose of the campaign, answer questions, and kindle enthusiasm. For maximum response, an experienced campaign director who can personally guide the effort is recommended. Nearly every church using this procedure testifies that the fee charged is repaid many times over by increased pledges and greater unity. If it is not possible to have a professional campaign director, the pastor and lay leaders should be prepared to commit major time to the effort and follow a proven resource guide.

After the church decides to make facility improvements, it should choose that fund-raising method which is most consistent with its understanding of the biblical concept of stewardship. If the need for financially realistic facility changes has been proven and members have participated fully in decision making, support is usually forthcoming to implement the project.

Borrowing Money for Construction

Following its intensive financial effort, the next step for the church is to seek preliminary loan commitments. To repeat what has been said before, the architect's work should now come to a halt until financing sufficient to complete the project is secured. Whether the church is dealing with a denominational loan officer or local banker, many questions will be asked. Those who approach lending institutions on behalf of the church should be armed with every possible fact to support their request. It is best to have all the information available for the first conference with a loan officer, with copies that can be left for review by the potential lenders. The church that comes prepared will save valuable time and have a better chance for an affirmative response. The type of data usually necessary is contained in the following list:

1. Survey facts, program goals, and other materials which indicate objectives of the church and the facility improvements necessary to help in reaching them. Also, list the schedule which has been followed and the votes received to indicate thoroughness of planning as well as support by the entire congregation.

2. The *net* Construction Budget including all estimated related expenses.

3. The architect's preliminary design, outline specifications, and cost estimate.

4. All details about current loans, mortgages, liens, and assessments; report on handling of loans paid within the past five years if there is no current loan.

5. Property and buildings owned by the church including dimensions of land (a recent survey, if available), cost and date of purchase, and previous building improvements.

6. Budget for the current year and results of pledging, if a general budget campaign was held.

7. Total church receipts and disbursements according to budget category for the past five years.

8. Monthly building fund receipts for the past three years; total now in the building fund with notation about where it is invested.

9. Results of the recent Capital Funds Campaign including number of pledges, length of pledging, average pledge, and total amount pledged.

10. Professional realtors' appraisal of property (if site or building purchase).

11. Articles of incorporation and bylaws of the church.

12. Church membership and average attendance (if not included in survey facts).

13. List of key congregational officers, such as pastor, treasurer,

       board and committee chairpersons, plus the church's attorney
       and architect.
  14. Denominational affiliations on the judicatory and national
       levels.
  15. Amount and length of loan requested.

Facts such as those included in the preceding list should be presented to potential lenders in the community and, if applicable, to the parent denominational body. While it may seem natural to approach the local bank, many churches borrow from their own denomination for a variety of reasons. Such national loan funds are handled with integrity and sound financial management. Sometimes the interest rate is favorable because of a revolving fund resulting from offerings designated for loans to churches. Thus, the interest charged is for administration of the loan fund plus some appreciation to keep pace with inflation. Other denominational funds which use investments from their members cannot charge extremely low interest rates.

Another reason for seeking denominational aid is that denominational leaders are very familiar with the churches and the way they operate. There is, naturally, strong support for the objectives of the church. This tends to make for good working relationships and can save time. Acquaintance of denominational loan officers with pastors and resource personnel is also an asset.

One other reason for approaching the national denomination is the possibility of access to additional resources, such as planning, program, building, and financial counsel. Such counsel can be extremely valuable to the church as it contemplates facility improvements. When communication with the denomination occurs and resources are shared in the early stages, confidence in the national agency usually builds and discussion about loans is a natural next step. In addition to banks, some savings and loan associations lend to churches. Other possibilities for loans include insurance companies and the pension funds of such organizations as labor unions, teachers' and public employees' associations. Two or more lending agencies may negotiate together to approve a participation loan. In such instances, each agency buys part interest in the loan and its security (1/2 or 1/3, for example) and receives the appropriate percentage of each monthly payment. One of the financial institutions serves as the lead lender and collector of payments from the church, distributing each share proportionately to other lenders according to the participation agreement. Thus, the process is not complicated for the borrowing church. There are many such participation loans now in existence between community banks and national denominational agencies.

When a potential lender is approached by a church with many facts supporting a feasible construction project, a straightforward positive or negative answer is usually given. However, sometimes statements are made which leave the church perplexed as to what is the real answer. One of these is: "Sorry, all our church money is already loaned out." Should this be the case, there is usually a related, correspondent bank nearby which the loan officer can contact for supplementary funds. This possibility or the participation loan described in the previous paragraph could be suggested to the bank.

Another statement occasionally heard is: "We will consider a loan, but all the church checking and savings accounts must be transferred here." The church may have no problem with this stipulation, but even so the transfer should not take place until after written assurance is received that the loan will be approved. A transfer of accounts may be a logical part of the total agreement, but not as a unilateral move required by the bank in order to give consideration to a loan. The merits of each lending possibility must be weighed carefully. Such a transfer of accounts allows the church less flexibility in the use of its funds. Interest rates need to be compared, too, in case they are lower than what might be paid elsewhere.

Still another statement heard on occasion is: "We will lend the money needed for construction but cannot provide permanent financing." This means that the loan covers the time of construction only. Such an arrangement usually does not meet the church's need. A construction-only loan should never be considered unless the source of permanent financing is assured. The process is more complicated and the cost usually higher when two loans are involved. This procedure should be followed only when the source of permanent financing can document that they will have the money by the projected date of construction completion. There could be some unusual but still valid reasons why that relatively short period of time would make a significant difference in lending capacity. Normally, however, a single loan at the time of construction for both construction and permanent financing is best.

One other statement made periodically is: "We will make a loan if the church has life insurance on the pastor equivalent to the principal balance throughout the amortization period." Typically, this is heard when a church has had rapid growth under the leadership of a popular pastor to whom there is great personal loyalty. Feeling that attendance and giving could decrease dramatically should this pastor die, the bank wants to protect its interest. Such a position is understandable and, in some cases, warranted. To protect another similar eventuality, one bank wanted the pastor to sign a statement that he would not leave that particular church for at least eight years. While these requirements may have validity in certain cases, again they should be compared with the stipulations of other potential lenders.

In discussing a possible church loan, officers from a certain bank mentioned nothing about any closing costs or charges for making their commitment. A later telephone call revealed that there would be several bank charges amounting to nearly 3 percent of the loan principal required by the church. Compared to other possibilities, the lending package offered by this bank had appeared quite favorable, but the additional 3 percent reversed that earlier judgment.

This experience is a reminder that the church needs to raise many important questions in its early negotiations with potential lenders. First is the subject of charges necessary to obtain a loan. There may be a service fee or a percentage of the loan (called "points") or both. The amount charged varies with the availability of mortgage funds. In typical supply and demand fashion, the charges will be higher if there is less money on hand to lend. (Most denominational lending agencies charge interest only, not service fees or points.) Another key question is whether or not the church has the privilege of prepayment without penalty. Some lenders have an additional charge if extra payments are made or if repayment comes ahead of schedule.

Still another question is whether the interest rate is set for the entire loan period or if the lender has the right to vary the rate according to economic conditions through the years. Under a variable interest plan, any rate adjustments are normally limited to once or twice a year at the most. The church usually has the option of refinancing elsewhere at those times if more favorable terms may be secured. A variation of this is, for example, a loan made on a twelve-year repayment schedule but with a note duration of four years. This means, in effect, that the lender is able to review the interest rate every few years. If interest percentages are expected to increase over the long term, it is more favorable to have a fixed rate. If they decrease, a variable rate that can move either up or down would be best.

When everything possible is known about the terms and conditions of the loan and the church has approved the most favorable offer, the lending institution will seek full documentation in accordance with its policies. These requirements are for the protection of both the lender and the church. The congregation will definitely need the assistance of an experienced attorney at this point. The following items are typical for full documentation:

1. Formal loan application form. (Also, recommendation of judicatory agency and statements by the church attorney about state laws applying to church loans if the financing is from a denominational source.)
2. Copy of Borrowing Resolution indicating vote of the church to borrow funds.
3. Certificate of election of church officers.
4. Articles of Incorporation, constitution, and bylaws of the church.
5. Note or Bond.
6. Recorded mortgage or deed of trust.
7. Policy of mortgage title insurance or title abstract.
8. Evidence of fire and extended insurance coverage.
9. Opinion of the church's attorney regarding loan documents.
10. Copy of the contract between the church and the architect.
11. Copy of the construction contract(s) and performance bond.
12. Copy of MAI appraisal (if purchase of property is involved).
13. Copy of the participation agreement (if more than one lender).

When documentation is completed satisfactorily, the loan is available for the congregation. In order to save interest costs, the church first uses the money it has accumulated to pay contractors. After these funds are exhausted, the lending agency is contacted. Requests for disbursements normally need to be supported by the contractor's monthly payment requests and an architect's certificate affirming that the work has been completed according to previously approved specifications and materials delivered as specified. Copies of lien waivers should be received from contractors as the work progresses.

Usually, there will be a retainage amount (such as 10 percent) withheld from each contractor's billing until the construction project is completed satisfactorily. This gives the church some leverage, if needed, should there be incomplete or unsatisfactory work. During construction, the church normally pays interest only on the accumulated monthly amounts disbursed. After the work is completed according to contract and the total loan amount has been utilized, constant monthly payments of principal and interest will begin.

Conclusion

This book has attempted to point out that wise stewardship of church, personal, and natural resources is more important today than ever before. A rising rate of inflation, needed new programs to minister to an ever more complex society, an awareness that natural resources are being depleted rapidly, and increasing competition for the time of those who give voluntary service to organizations like the church all impinge to create the resource crises. Congregations, therefore, need to take a hard look at their priorities and use as much as possible of every dollar for ministries to people in the name of Christ.

Since the provision of an ecclesiastical building has traditionally required major time, energy, and money, much of the content of the book has centered upon ways that these resources can be conserved. Acceptance and implementation of many of the "different" concepts contained herein will not come easily. On the one hand, the national economy is not yet to the point where the pressure for conservation is strong enough to cause precipitous action; on the other hand, too few Christians interpret biblical concepts of stewardship so literally as to believe these concepts should be applied on their own merit regardless of contemporary circumstances. While the latter motivation is best, it may take general economic change to bring widespread action. As the time for major change inevitably approaches, it is hoped that this small volume will make some contribution to the more effective utilization of church resources.

Appendix A

Survey Report Outline

This is an outline of the facts to be collected by the Data-Gathering Task Group.

I. THE CHURCH

A. Brief historical background

B. Membership

1. Current resident membership and annual fluctuations over the past 10 to 20 years.

2. Membership gain and loss table for a 10- to 20-year period: gains by baptism, letter, experience, etc., and losses by death, letter, erasure, etc.

3. Age and sex of resident members and comparison of the age-sex distribution pattern of the church with that of the community: also, a separate age-sex breakdown of those who have joined the church during the past two years.

4. Location of the residence of members in relationship to the church building: under 1 mile, 1 to 2 miles, etc.

5. Means by which people reach the church building: walk, public transportation, auto (with own family or with others), etc.; also, the percentage of adults who travel at least 10 miles each way to work.

6. Length of time that members have belonged to the church, in five-year categories; also, determine the approximate date which marks the break between the newest one-half and the oldest one-half of the membership.

7. A comparison of the changes in church membership with community population changes.

8. Determine why at least the leadership group (officers, boards, committees) became members of this particular congregation (preaching, family ties, friends, location, specific programs, etc.) and list the percentages according to those categories.

9. Percentage of adult members who work outside the home.

C. Attendance

1. Yearly average attendance in both worship and church school for the past 10 to 20 years and a comparison of those attendances.

2. Monthly average attendance in both worship and church school for the past 3 years.

3. Enrollment and average attendance for each church school class during the past year; also, "highest days" attendance for the past year (this is the average of the two highest Sundays from the nine highest months of the year); added to this chart could be the recommended square footage/pupil ratio and the total space now utilized by each class.

4. List all other program functions sponsored by the church, their frequency of meeting, and average attendance for the past five years (midweek and evening services, Scouts, VBS, mission society, dinners, etc.). List whether meeting in church building or elsewhere.

D. Finances

1. Total income and expenditures for the past 5 to 10 years, with a breakdown into categories, such as general fund, missions, building fund, etc. Note if the church has had an every-member pledging effort and what special appeals have been made, such as a Capital Funds Campaign.

2. Comparison of the total income trend with fluctuations in the per capita or per family income of the area over the past 10 years.

3. Profile of giving, showing the number and percentage of givers in each category of offering-per-week, such as 0—$1, $1—$3, $3—$5, etc.

4. Statement of present mortgage indebtedness position and record of repayment, if any.

5. Cost of building repairs and maintenance for the past 5 years.

E. Present Facilities

1. Plot plan of land owned by the church, giving dimensions, locations of buildings, driveways, parking areas (including off-street parking capacity), etc.

2. Floor plans of building(s) showing all program areas and supporting spaces. Either on the plan or on a separate page with a key back to the plan, it should be indicated what group meets in the space and the square footage.

3. Engineer's report showing condition of facilities.

4. Inventory of all furniture and equipment owned by the church, with an indication of that which is serviceable and that which needs replacement.

F. Program "specialities" of the congregation: goals set last year and record of achievement.

G. List the other studies, surveys, or consultations that have been conducted by persons outside of the church membership during the past 10 years, including the date, leader, and results of the study.

H. Interviews of church members.

I. Comparative membership/participation ratios of area churches.

II. THE COMMUNITY

A. Brief historical background

B. Population

1. Past trends: fluctuations over the past 20–30 years.

2. Present population details and factors in future population changes: predictions of planning agencies.

3. Characteristics of the population: factors such as the level of education, size of families, ethnic makeup, percentage of homeowners, etc.

C. Economic Development

1. Employment characteristics: list by classification, number and percentage of the total labor force—professional, technical, farmer, manager, clerical, laborers, etc.

2. Predicted future trends in employment.

D. Land Use

1. Present and projected land use, including location and pattern of land development for residential, commercial, multifamily and industrial purposes, and also possible annexations.

2. Transportation patterns: existing major arteries and feeder streets, and planning projections for future streets and highways.

3. Zoning and building code requirements for new church construction and remodeling, including off-street parking requirements.

E. Schools, Parks, and Recreation

1. Present and projected school locations.

2. School enrollment trends, past, present and future, particularly within the neighborhood of the church building.

3. Present and proposed parks and public facilities, including both indoor and outdoor recreational areas.

F. Other churches in the neighborhood, their location and distance from your church building

G. Interviews of community leaders and organizations

Appendix B

Formula for Energy Efficiency Ratio

1) Total size of building in cubic feet (width x length x ceiling height). Determine for each room (including hallways) and add together to obtain the total building space: _____ cubic feet

2) Obtain from the Weather Bureau or local newspaper the heating degree days[1] of the area for either one specific winter month or for an entire year:

   _____ heating degree days per _____ (time)

3) For *this same period of time,* secure from the treasurer or fuel supplier the amount of fuel consumed and multiply it by the conversion factor below to obtain the Btu's (British thermal units) used:

   gallons #2 heating oil x 140,000 equals _____ Btu's

   _____ therms natural gas x 100,000 equals __ Btu's

   _____ kilowatt-hours electricity x 3,400 equals __ Btu's

---

[1] The heating degree days represent the number of degrees below 65 the average temperature is each day of the heating season. If the average temperature one day is 40 degrees, for example, 25 heating degree days are added for that day.

4) Divide the Btu's used by the cubic feet of space to determine the amount of heat required for each cubic foot during the month or year.

$$\frac{\text{Btu's/mo. or year}}{\text{cubic feet}}$$

equals _____ Btu's/cu. ft/
mo. or yr.

5) Divide this figure by the heating degree days *for the same period of time* to obtain the EER:

$$\frac{\text{Btu's/cu.ft./mo. or yr.}}{\text{ht. deg. days/mo. or yr.}}$$

equals _____Btu's/cu. ft/
htg. deg. day
(EER)

Appendix C

Checklist for Reducing Fuel Use in Church Buildings [1]

The amount of fuel used to heat a building is directly related to the building heat load, expressed in British Thermal Units (Btu's) and the temperature difference ($\triangle T$) between inside and outside, and inversely related to the combustion value of the fuel (C) and the efficiency of the heating plant (E).

$$\text{Fuel used} = \frac{\text{Btu's} \times \triangle T}{C \times E}$$

1. INCREASE HEATING SYSTEM EFFICIENCY

All these measures will affect the entire fuel usage for the whole year; if a significant improvement is made here, it is likely to be most cost-effective.

Heating Plant — Have combustion efficiency of burner checked by fuel supplier or heating contractor.

Distribution System — Check distribution system: fans, pumps, valves, dampers, etc. In buildings with complex heating and ventilating systems, consult a mechanical engineer.

Cycling — Is the heating plant cycling on and off more frequently than necessary? Check with heating contractor.

[1] *Energy Stewardship,* © copyright 1977 by Total Environmental Action, Inc., Harrisville, NH 03450. Used by permission.

Stack Dampers can save heat which would otherwise escape up the chimney.

2. REDUCE TEMPERATURE DIFFERENCE

If the heat can be turned down in unused spaces, fuel is saved.

Zoning Is it possible, with the present system, to turn down the heat in spaces which are not being used, without affecting spaces which are being used? Consult a heating contractor or mechanical engineer about rezoning where necessary.

Scheduling Can the present use schedule be changed so that temperatures can be kept down in more spaces? This means changing use patterns to adapt to the building rather than changing the building to adapt to use patterns.

Timing of Setbacks If it takes time for spaces to heat up, use automatic timers to control temperature settings. With timer, fuel will not be wasted by turning up the heat sooner than it is needed, or forgetting to set it back when it's not.

Hot Water Reducing hot water temperature setting will save energy. Automatic timers can raise settings for periods of heavy use.

3. REDUCE THE BUILDING LOAD

The rate at which a building loses heat is higher during the times when it is being heated. If temperatures are set back for long periods, insulation loses its cost-effectiveness. Insulate first in areas which are heated most.

Insulation Walls, floor, roofs, and ceilings can be insulated either by filling cavities or adding rigid insulation and new finish. Consult a building contractor.

Windows Storm windows tend to be less cost-effective than insulation because of their higher cost. If shutters and curtains can be made airtight, they will reduce infiltration.

Caulk and Weather-strip Reduce infiltration of cold air around window and door cracks. Be aware of expected life as well as initial cost in comparing types.

4. SOLAR ENERGY

South-facing walls and roofs can be retrofitted to maximize solar heat gain. These devices will become more cost-effective as the cost of fossil fuels rises.

Appendix D

Cost Pay-back Periods

Example: —Original cost (Co) of insulation and storm windows is $4,400 plus $600 interest on a three-year loan for a total of $5,000.

—Cost savings (Cs) of the above, estimated by an engineer to be $400 for the first year. (Without taking inflation into account, the "straight" pay-back would be $5,000 divided by $400, or 12½ years.)

—Estimated average future fuel inflation rate (r) is 10% per year. (Many studies have been made recently by utilities companies and the government. The type of fuel involved and geographical location of the church are both important. While some fuels are costing as much as 35% more each year, a conservative national estimate used here is 10%. In the example, this rate is expressed by the decimal figure 0.10.)

—The number of years (N) for the improvement to pay for itself **with inflation accounted for** is found by using this formula:

$$N = \frac{\log \ r \ \dfrac{Co}{Cs} + (1 + r)}{\log \ (1 + r)} - 1$$

Log stands for logarithm. This is a term from high school algebra which is often forgotten by graduation time. However, an engineer or high school math teacher will be able to help. After the addition, multiplication, and division of the formula have been completed, look in the simple log table of an algebra book for the correct numbers. Then divide one more time, subtract one, and there is the answer. For this example, the formula will look like this:

$$N = \frac{\log 0.10 \quad \frac{\$5,000}{\$400} + 1.10}{\log 1.10} - 1 = \frac{\log 2.35}{\log 1.10} - 1$$

$$= \frac{0.3711}{0.0414} - 1 = 8.96 - 1 = \underline{7.96 \text{ years}}$$

In this case, if annual fuel inflation averages 10%, the added insulation and storm windows will pay for themselves in a little less than 8 years. (Note the 4.5 year shorter pay-back period when the inflation factor is included.) From that point on, the continuing fuel savings can be reallocated to needed church programs. If inflation actually averages 15% per year, pay-back will come in 6.92 years; or in 6.17 years if the inflation rate averages 20%. The same formula will indicate pay-back periods for potential fuel saving measures in new construction.

Appendix E

Construction Budget

The resource side of a church construction budget may look something like this:

1. **Building Funds**
   - *a.* Savings funds and certificates $_____
   - *b.* Stocks, current value $_____
   - *c.* Bonds, current value $_____
   - *d.* Cash $_____
   - *e.* Other $_____
   -   Total Building Funds $_____

2. **Projected income until completion of construction**
   - *a.* Current average monthly Building Fund
     income $_____
     Months until CFC (Capital Funds Campaign)   x_____
       + $_____
   - *b.* Estimated average monthly income after CFC $_____
     Months from CFC until construction completion x_____
       + $_____

   Total Additional Building Funds expected before
   completion of construction   = $_____

3. **Maximum borrowing potential** (Use whichever method is considered most accurate *or* two or more methods and divide to

obtain the average *or* some other method that is appropriate to the situation, and realistic.)

a. Estimated total annual church income, all funds, including income from building financial effort, if held:

$$\$\underline{\hspace{2cm}} \times 35\% = \$\underline{\hspace{2cm}}$$

This is the annual repayment ability of the church and gives the 15 year loan amount when multiplied by 8[1]:

Annual church income x 35% x 8 = $\$\underline{\hspace{2cm}}$

b. Estimated pledge results, 3 year CFC $\$\underline{\hspace{2cm}}$

$$\times 2\frac{1}{2}[1]$$

$$= \$\underline{\hspace{2cm}}$$

c. Estimated annual Building Fund income during the life of the loan

$$\$\underline{\hspace{2cm}}$$

$$\times 8[1]$$

$$= \$\underline{\hspace{2cm}}$$

d. Other $\$\underline{\hspace{2cm}}$

If using more than one method, <u>AVERAGE</u>

Maximum Borrowing Potential $\$\underline{\hspace{2cm}}$

4. Estimated income from sale of property $\$\underline{\hspace{2cm}}$

other $\$\underline{\hspace{2cm}}$

Total $\$\underline{\hspace{2cm}}$

Summary of Resources

1. Current Building Funds $\$\underline{\hspace{2cm}}$
2. Additional Building Funds to constr. completion $\$\underline{\hspace{2cm}}$
3. Maximum Borrowing Potential $\$\underline{\hspace{2cm}}$
4. Income from Sale of Property, etc. $\$\underline{\hspace{2cm}}$
5. Other $\$\underline{\hspace{2cm}}$

Total Estimated Building Resources $\$\underline{\hspace{2cm}}$

---

[1] These figures assume a 15-year loan amortization period. For 12 years, multiply by 7 in "a" and "c" and by 2¼ in "b"; for 10 years, multiply by 6 in "a" and "c" and by 2 in "b". These multipliers (8, 7, etc.) are suggested because the result of their use will be an amount necessary for loan repayment, assuming an annual interest rate of 8½% to 9½%.

Related Expenses

The expense part of a church construction budget might include the following items:

1. Professional Expenses
   a. Architectural & Engineering fees $_____
   b. Legal Expenses $_____
   c. Planning Consultant's fees $_____
   d. Financial Consultant/CFC fee $_____
      Total Professional Expenses $_____

2. Furnishings & Equipment Expenses
   a. Furnishings, Sanctuary $_____
   b. Other Furnishings $_____
   c. Equipment $_____
   d. Organ $_____
      Total for Furnishings & Equipment $_____

3. Demolition & Property Expenses
   a. Demolition $_____
   b. Property Purchase $_____
      Total $_____

4. Miscellaneous Expenses
   a. Topographical Survey $_____
   b. Soil Testing $_____
   c. Insurance during constr. $_____
   d. Interest during constr. $_____
   e. Landscaping $_____
   f. Other _____ $_____
      Total Misc. Expenses $_____

5. Contingencies
   a. Inflation $_____
   b. Omitted Items $_____
      Total $_____

Summary of Expenses

1. Professional Expenses $\$$_____
2. Furnishings & Equipment Expenses $\$$_____
3. Demolition & Property Expenses $\$$_____
4. Miscellaneous Expenses $\$$_____
5. Contingencies $\$$_____

                 Total Estimated Expenses $\$$_____

Total Estimated Building Resources $\$$_____
Less Total Estimated Expenses $\$$_____

                 Net Construction Budget $\$$_____

Selected Bibliography

Abernethy, William B., *A New Look for Sunday Morning.* Nashville: Abingdon Press, 1975. A case study about a church with a unique Sunday morning worship format—the theological and educational rationale behind a wholistic approach.

AIA Research Corp. for HUD, *Solar Dwelling Design Concepts.* Washington, D.C.: U.S. Government Printing Office, Assistant Printer, Supt. of Documents (#023-000-033401)

Anderson, Bruce; and Riordan, Michael, *The Solar Home Book: Heating, Cooling, and Designing with the Sun.* Harrisville, N.H.: Chesire Books, 1976.

_____, *Solar Energy: Fundamentals in Building Design.* New York: McGraw-Hill, 1977.

Anderson, Philip and Phoebe, *The House Church.* Nashville: Abingdon Press, 1975. The goals, functions, and methods of the house church.

Baumann, Dan, *All Originality Makes a Dull Church.* Santa Ana, Calif.: Vision House, 1976. "Success" stories of several effective churches pointing out transferable characteristics and essential ingredients.

Belknap, Ralph; and Critz, Richard, *Shared Facilities: The Mankato Center.* King of Prussia, Pa.: Religious Publishing Company, 1977. The story of three congregations (Baptist, Methodist, UCC) sharing one building.

Clark, Wilson, *Energy for Survival: The Alternative to Extinction.* New York: Doubleday & Co., Inc., Anchor Press, 1974. A very scholarly treatise on the present energy situation and new alternatives, such as solar, wind, and others.

Cobb, John B., Jr., *Is It Too Late? A Theology of Ecology.* Encino, Calif.: Glencoe Press, 1971. This book presents a theological perspective of ecology. Cobb presents a thesis that people are part of the ecological system and that they are participants rather than stewards. As participants, there are new perspectives and opportunities within the relationship.

Commoner, Barry, *The Poverty of Power.* New York: Alfred A. Knopf, Inc., 1976.

Crowther, Richard, *Sun Earth: How to Apply Free Energy Sources to Our Homes and Buildings.* Denver: Crowther/Solar Group, 1976. A well-illustrated book for those wishing to improve their background understanding of the use of the environment as related to buildings.

Darrow, Ken; and Pam, Rick, *Appropriate Technology Sourcebook.* Stanford, Calif.: Volunteers in Asia, Publishers, 1976. A sourcebook on technology from underdeveloped countries.

Evans, J. Bruce, *Experiments in Church, The Story of Fellowship.* Baton Rouge, La.: Fellowship Church, 136 So. Acadian Throughway. The story of an experimental, ecumenical church in operation since 1963.

Fenhagen, James C., *Mutual Ministry: New Vitality for the Local Church.* New York: The Seabury Press, Inc., 1977. A new approach to the problems of ministry and some insights into its changing needs.

Finnerty, Adam Daniel, *No More Plastic Jesus: Global Justice and Christian Lifestyle.* New York: Orbis Books, 1977.

Freeman, S. David, *Energy: The New Era.* New York: Vintage Press, 1974. Freeman leads the reader through an in-depth study of the energy crisis from its causes to future alternatives. He discusses the factors that impinge on solution: ecological, economical, social, and political. Freeman maintains that part of the solution is a change in American life-style.

Fritsch, Albert J.; and Castleman, Barry I., *Lifestyle Index.* Published by the Center for Science in the Public Interest, 1779 Church St., NW, Washington, DC 20036. 60 pages. An interesting focus on how energy consumption relates to individuals; allows you to take a look at your own energy use patterns.

Fritsch, Albert J. et al, eds., *Ninety-Nine Ways to a Simple Lifestyle.* The Center for Science in the Public Interest. Garden City, N.Y.: Anchor Books, 1977. Covers many practical subjects about conservation.

Gladden, Richard K.; Green, Norman M., Jr.; and Rusbuldt, Richard E., *The Local Church Planning Manual.* Valley Forge: Judson Press, 1977. A comprehensive planning guide including several optional procedures.

Johnson, Douglas W., *Managing Change in the Church*, New York: Friendship Press, 1974. Factors that make change necessary and ways to participate in constructive change.

Leckie, Jim; Masters, Gil; Whitehouse, Harry; and Young, Lily, *Other Homes and Garbage.* Published by Sierra Club Books, 530 Bush Street, San Francisco, CA 94108, 1975. 302 pages.

Salter, Petruschell, and Wolf, *Energy Conservation in Nonresidential Buildings.* NSF, The Rand Corporation, 1976.

Schumacher, E. F., *Small Is Beautiful: Economics As If People Mattered.* New York: Harper & Row, Publishers, 1973.

Scully, Prowler, Anderson, and Mahone, *The Fuel Savers: A Kit of Solar Ideas for Existing Homes.* Harrisville, N.H.: Total Environmental Action, 1975.

Spies, Konzo, Calvin, and Thoms, *350 Ways to Save Energy (and Money).* New York: Crown Publishers. One of the most practical books around that pragmatically explains energy concepts and how an individual can reduce his/her energy consumption now in cost effective ways.

Van Dresser, Peter, *Home Grown Sun Dwellings.* Santa Fe, Calif.: Jene Lyon, Publisher, 1977. An excellent book on the direct passive-gain solar building.

Wallace, Daniel, *Energy We Can Live With.* Emmaus, Pa.: Rodale

Press, 1976. This book covers a broad spectrum of energy-related concerns in a nontechnical way.

Watson, Donald, *Designing and Building a Solar Home: Your Place in the Sun.* Charlotte, Vt.: Garden Way Publishing, 1977.

Index

Acoustical requirements, 45-46, 55, 57, 72-73
Architects, selection criteria, 83-85, 131, 134-135

Backup energy systems, 93, 108
Bond sales, 141-143
Budget, construction, 130-138, 165-168

Capital Funds Campaigns, 131-132, 135, 143-145
Commercial space, utilization of, 50-52
Costs, space usage, 58, 123

Data gathering, 20-21
Day-care programs, 70-71
Decision-making procedures, 16-17

Educational space, 64, 68-73
Energy Efficiency Ratio, 80-81, 159-160
Energy, survey of buildings, 78-82, 161-162
Engineering feasibility study, 125-126

Fellowship-narthex space, 46-47, 65-69

Handicapped, accessibility for, 116
House-churches, 47-50

Libraries, 68-72
Loan criteria, 128-130, 132, 136-137, 144-150

Master planning, 44-45, 47,
Movable seating and furnishings, 55, 61-63, 135-136
Multiple sessions, 40-43

Nursery school, 71

Open classrooms, 72-73
Organization for planning, 19

Participation of members, 25-26
Phased construction, 44-47
Pledging, 143-144
Prioritizing options, 26-27
Programming, 21-25

Recommendations, preparation of, 27-30
Recreational space, 65-67
Renovating church buildings, 124-126

Sacred-secular spaces, 54, 60-61
Sale of church property, 132-134
Shared facilities, 31-37, 50-52
Simultaneous sessions, 42-43
Site orientation, 85-87
Solar collectors, 95-99
Solar energy, passive, 95-97, 107-108
Solar-heated churches, 99-108
Solar insolation, 94

Time scheduling, 18, 127-129, 139-140

Underground buildings, 88-89

Worship space, 60-65